"In the decade I've had Bobby as my coach, I've not only enjoyed a long and successful career with his innovative coaching methods, but I've continually been inspired and motivated by his ability to always discover the good in everything. His holistic approach and passionate attention to the mental aspects of running are the cornerstones on which I have built my career. He discovers and draws out of me performances I would never have believed possible. His seminars and his book, **Magical Running: A unique path to running fulfillment** *will greatly benefit all levels of runners."*

- COLLEEN DE REUCK
TWO-TIME OLYMPIAN
WORLD RECORD HOLDER AT 10-MILES AND 20-KILOMETERS

"When my runners come to the lab for physiological testing and we devote a few days to figuring out 'what makes them tick,' there are three questions I ask that tend to be the most difficult: Tell me your long-term goals, tell me your short-term goals, and tell me the present level of your commitment. The answers to these questions set the stage for an athlete's moving forward—all the fitness in the world is worth nothing if there isn't a plan for the future, based upon one's desires.

Bobby Mc Gee's **Magical Running: A unique path to running fulfillment** *is by far the best approach that I have seen to help runners of all abilities deal effectively with these delicate and difficult questions. If one 'gets it together mentally' then the physical work of training becomes a joyful effort, and the inevitable result is 'successful fitness,' in which one's dreams of excellence and passion for getting there bring reality to the experience. Runners will really find this book helpful, and the quicker they start reading it, the quicker they'll start improving!"*

- PROF. DAVID MARTIN
US OLYMPIC COMMITTEE LONG DISTANCE PHYSIOLOGY COORDINATOR
USA TRACK & FIELD LONG DISTANCE DEVELOPMENT COORDINATOR

"Bobby Mc Gee has come up with a splendid summary plan for running success, even more powerful and compelling than Maxwell Maltz's Psycho-Cybernetics prescription for positive thinking. Methodically, Mc Gee instructs how achieving a positive focus will lead to success, and how to counteract those negatives that have proved impediments to us all. Employing his well thought out, holistic approach to running success is a must for those wishing to gain the racer's edge ."

- PAUL CHRISTMAN
EDITOR OF RUNNING STATS INTERNATIONAL RESULTS NEWSLETTER
AUTHOR OF "THE PURPLE RUNNER"

MAGICAL RUNNING

A unique path to running fulfillment

BOBBY MC GEE

FOREWORDS BY FRANK SHORTER AND LORRAINE MOLLER

BOBBYSEZ
PUBLISHING

Bobbysez Publishing
Boulder, Colorado

Magical Running:
A unique path to running fulfillment

Published by Bobbysez Publishing.
Your comments and suggestions are valued.

For permissions, comments and questions please write to the publisher at Bobbysez Publishing, P.O. Box 17866, Boulder, CO 80308-0866.
Telephone: 877 9 MAGICAL, email: info@magicalife.com,
Website: www.magicalife.com

To order additional copies of this book, please find the order blank at the end of the book.

Publisher's Cataloging-in-Publication
(Provided by Quality Books, Inc.)

Mc Gee, Bobby
    Magical running : a unique path to running
fulfillment / Bobby Mc Gee. -- 1st ed.
    p. cm.
    ISBN : 1-930499-00-0

    1. Running--Psychological aspects.
    2. Motivation (Psychology) I. Title

GV1061.8.P75M34 2000   796.42
                         QBI00-248

Editors: Dagny Scott, Tony Longhurst
Cover design: Robert Howard
Illustrations: Dale Crawford
Layout: Remmert Design

Printed in the United States on recycled paper.

**BOBBYSEZ
PUBLISHING**

Most definitely for Colleen

...from willing guinea pig

to queen of the roads –

you are a superstar

Colleen de Reuck is a success story whose brilliance was strongly influenced by Bobby Mc Gee's coaching and motivational skills.

I believe it is not the training,

but the spaces between the training

that are the most critical.

- BOBBY MC GEE

CONTENTS

UNLEASH THE RUNNER WITHIN

ACKNOWLEDGEMENTS

I can't recall how many years it's been since I first realized I wanted to write a book, but it has been one of the sources of the driving passion I have for living my life to the fullest.

My writing, my lectures and seminars would not have had wings as broad, nor flight as breathtaking had it not been for my friend and colleague, my happy slave-driver, my motivator and always-believer, Tony Longhurst.

Thanks Tone. Know always that without you all this would have remained only a dream.

As always with a project of this nature there are so many incredible people involved. If I have left a name out, forgive me. Go out and run off your frustration!

My sincere thanks to the following for their expert input and effort: Arturo Barrios, Joan Benoit-Samuelson, Amby Burfoot, Paul Christman, Beth Darnell, Colleen De Reuck, Sally Edwards, Bruce Fordyce, Jacqueline Gareau, Johnny Halberstadt, Barbara Heubner, George Hirsch, Gordon Irving, Don Kardong, Dave Martin, Carolyn Mather, Lorraine Moller, Zola Pieterse, Mark Plaatjes, Brendan Reilly, Toni Reavis, Ric Rojas, Carl Rose, Hal Rothman, Kelly Ryan, Steve Scott, Frank Shorter, Jon Sinclair, Priscilla Welch, David Whitman and Maryanne Young.

Also my sincere appreciation to Dagny Scott; no book could go to print without the knowledgeable eye of a fine editor.

And finally to my athletes: Thank you for being my greatest teachers. You gave me my life through allowing me to serve.

Homata Hantle   (Sotho for "run well")

FOREWORDS

Throw away your ten-function chronometer, heart-rate monitor with the computer printout, training log, orthotics, high-tech underwear, pace charts and laboratory-rat-tested, air-injected, gel-lined, motion-controlled, top-of-the-line, fashion footwear.

Run with only your imagination. It is your rich companion guiding you into realms further and faster and more daring than you ever dreamed.

Follow it through exotic lands in far-off galaxies in times past and future. Run with the lithe strides of the Kalahari bushmen in the hunt for dinner, or in the thundering midst of a stampede of elephants. When you are thirsty run toward the oasis in Death Valley at midday, and when you are in front, run as if you are hunted by a tribe of hungry cannibals.

Sometimes giant strides with giant feet that cover whole countries can be very economical. And when the ground is boggy, launch off each foot to pluck a star from the heavens and carry the lightness of them in your pockets. Uphill, attach a few helium balloons to your vest so that your feet skim the ground, leaving no footprints. Downhills are free energy, so take off the brakes and spread your wings for take-off.

In stiff competition cast a line to the person in front and gently reel yourself in so that they never notice. Then, as you slip past, become as invisible as a colorless rainbow and as silent as lightning that outran its thunder. And when you cross the finish line, always throw your arms in the air in total ecstasy. After all, this is your running and your life. Come on, you have to admit that there is nothing like that feeling, knowing you are the master of your running destiny. No limits, just you and as far as your mind can stretch.

In this sparkling book Bobby shows all runners how to have magical lives. There is nothing else worth running for.

- **LORRAINE MOLLER**
  1992 OLYMPIC MARATHON BRONZE MEDALLIST
  4-TIME OLYMPIAN

I have known Bobby for many years and closely observed the way he implements and communicates his coaching theory. My conclusion is that he is one of the best around at blending the mental and physical aspects of training and racing.

His work with Josia Thugwane, the 1996 Olympic Marathon champion, and Colleen De Reuck, one of the world's all-time great road racers, speaks for itself. He truly understands the need for an athlete to maintain a mindset that is holistic, flexible and adaptable.

To me, "magical" means creating a realistic, mental image of yourself and integrating it into your physical training program. Here, Bobby clearly lays out the paths that can be taken to maximize the possibilities for success. He has a unique ability to explain his theory in a way that is easy to understand and chronicle.

*This makes **Magical Running** a guide that can truly benefit runners at all levels of ability.*

- **FRANK SHORTER**
  1972 OLYMPIC MARATHON GOLD MEDALLIST
  1976 OLYMPIC MARATHON SILVER MEDALLIST

INTRODUCTION

UNLEASH THE BEST RUNNER YOU CAN BE

Does your running occur by accident? Are you sometimes puzzled that your efforts leave you unfulfilled, despite regular training?

Creating your running through striving only for better physical performances is highly limiting and can be hollow and frustrating.

It is possible instead to create your running exactly as you desire, each step of the way.

This book is a unique guide to a total and complete running experience.

Why go to all the effort and expense of training your body for an optimum performance, only to have it be sabotaged by negative, haphazard and ineffectual thinking?

There is another way, and this is it!

By following along with these pages you will be guided in a powerful and effective process of creating outstanding running experiences. You will gain more from your training efforts and are guaranteed of a performance on race day that will meet and more likely exceed any expectations you might have had.

Lace up your mental running shoes and let's go for the runs of your life!

CREATING MAGIC

HOW AND WHY THIS RUNNING PATH?

"Fortune favors the prepared mind."
-LOUIS PASTEUR

When you begin with running, the first thing on your mind is usually to get fit enough to either compete, or to enjoy a level of conditioning beyond that which you started out with. This is of course a never-ending process, only you don't know it at the time! Many runners never reach a point where they consider that perhaps further improvement might involve something other than just training harder or more scientifically.

Some runners do realize that improvement both in physical performance and in the quality of the experience can be gained through applying themselves "mentally" too. These runners often do so by believing that perhaps there is something wrong with their thinking. They then set about trying to repair this "problem". What they strive for, is a return to "normal", so that they can begin afresh, without this ineffectual thinking holding them back.

It's not often you hear a runner say something like this: "I've accomplished every-thing I ever wanted to as a runner." Or this: "I know I've reached my athletic potential." That's because most runners experience the frustration of knowing what they wish to do or are capable of, while never being able to achieve this desired level.

Runners fall short of their hopes and dreams for any number of reasons. Solving training problems can be relatively simple. Increase or decrease mileage, add interval workouts, and the like. But how does one "fix" a lack of confidence? Or motivation? The roadblocks most runners face have more to do with the mind than the miles, and these challenges are much more complicated to solve than rearranging a training log.

When an athlete is faced with such a mental block, traditional sport psychology attempts to pinpoint a breakdown in thinking and then to identify its cause. Once the cause has been determined, the stumbling block can be removed and the results of the "malfunction" can be "healed." What the traditional practitioner strives for, is a return to "normal," so that the "patient" or athlete can begin afresh, without the burden of this past malfunction holding them back.

However, another approach is to create an entirely new plan for the future. This book explains in detail how to go about designing and installing this plan. Now being used with great success by top performers, this relatively recent mode of thinking is based wholly upon what is possible for the performer. While the past is acknowledged, it is granted less significance in setting up a future plan of action. Instead of changing an existing way of thinking, it is replaced with a new one.

In general, when you take on the challenge of recreating your running, you are faced with these two approaches:

- identify what didn't work and attempt to change the bits and pieces, so that it does work, or
- replace the old ways with entirely new habits.

The danger of using the first—traditional method—is that you are using the base material of what essentially did not work to create something that just might. A high risk indeed, as you remain stuck in a malfunctioning mindset. Too often no amount of patching, changing and altering can bring about deep, effective, meaningful growth.

The second method provides a powerful opportunity for a fresh paradigm, a clean slate with which to begin. Experience and lessons are brought along from past successes, but without the ailments. This method operates from the understanding that there is nothing wrong, but rather that something new can be created.

The process isn't unlike what you might have gone through when, as a young adult, you realized you could become whomever you choose to be. As a young child you were unconscious of the factors that formed you. Your parents, friends, teachers, cultural background, schooling, social standing and other environmental factors, as well as genetics, determine this "first creation" of yourself. But eventually as an adult—hopefully—you come to realize that how you are, is not who you are! With this understanding comes the realization that you have not been condemned to a life of being this "you" that you accidentally became as a result of circumstance. You can be whomever you choose to be.

Such change doesn't come easily. It requires constant effort, patience and practice. But the rewards of joy and fulfillment greatly supersede the effort. And in the end you have created a life of choice and influence. Compare this to a reactive life of being a victim of circumstance and concern!

Similarly, with your sport, you have assembled your running legacy unconsciously, influenced by many factors not chosen by you and by events that occurred along the way. It is important to note that there really is no wrong or right way in which your running developed—only the way in which it did develop, and how you feel about it. If you are reading this book, there must already be much about your running that is successful and that can be used to further enhance your running experiences. By setting off on this new path, you'll find that your running can provide all it used to, and a level of experience and enjoyment beyond what you thought possible.

What lies ahead is a journey of discovery of how your running is, and then the fulfilling process of determining what it is you want from your running, how you plan to gain access to that, and finally how to remain committed and in action with this chosen process.

Not everyone has the opportunity, good fortune or talent to be noticed and helped upon the right path. Although all top athletes achieved what they did through their own endeavors, they were guided in some special way.

Arturo Barrios, one of the finest of the world-class runners to come out of that mecca of distance running, Mexico, had the following to say in this regard:

"Some people say champions are born and others say champions are made, but I believe it's a little of both. You obviously have to be born with the right physical abilities, but then you have to work on the mental abilities.

"I was fortunate enough to be born with physical talent and then to have a good high school coach who started me off on the right track. Early on my coach explained to me that running fast was going to take discipline and consistency over many years. For me it became a challenge to find out how fast I was going to run a 10K: Was I good enough to run 28 minutes or 27 minutes?

"It was a challenge I would face over the next several years by paying great care to my training. The bottom line is that to find out what you are made of, you have to be very disciplined when it comes to training every single day, twice a day, six out of seven days a week. That kind of discipline is what led to my success. And in my case, being from Mexico, making that kind of choice was a way getting out of poverty, a way to get an education. So for me, discipline was my choice. I knew it was what would make my running a ticket to another life.

"Running in Boulder one day with a group of world class runners, we passed a statue in a park that everyone touched as they ran by. 'Why are you doing that?' I asked. 'For good luck' they said. I thought about that and after a while I answered them: 'I train for good luck.'"

Arturo is a one-time 10,000-meter world record holder, and winner and record holder of countless of the world's greatest road races.

Much of a runner's frustration is caused by not ever really being able to achieve a desired level of performance, despite knowing what they are capable of, or wish to do. This book, like Arturo's coaches, provides a practical map to discovering that path and how to remain upon it.

HOW TO BEST USE THIS BOOK

There are 12 major areas in this book through which you can create a lifetime of magical running and also individual races and events. Although you need not follow the specific order in which these 12 areas are presented, doing so may be helpful.

Each concept is presented in theory and supported by anecdotes from some of the world's greatest athletes. You will then be guided through a series of practical questions to discover your own unique recipe for running fulfillment. Examples are provided to assist you, both within the text and at the end of each chapter.

In the following pages you will discover a method by which you can take control of the elusive elements essential to your running success (which you already use in some form or another). By mastering these components, you will be able to guide your thoughts and subsequent actions to support your physical endeavors to the maximum.

The value of such an approach lies in the self-discovery that comes from a deep questioning of one's motives and intent. This process will provide subsequent insight and control of the components in your running. This in turn will lead to ongoing joy and fulfillment throughout your running career.

There is much to be gained from consistently completing these exercises. By doing so you will discover and rediscover the elements in your running that make it the activity that excites and inspires you. Keep the following points in mind to ensure that you gain maximum value from each section, and from the book in its entirety:

- **Your wishes, desires and perspectives will continually change.** This is human nature and therefore it would be most effective if you regularly (once per week, or at least once per month) reassess and recreate each of the 12 areas presented. When you become aware of how much more is to be gained from running, you will continually discover new levels to which you aspire. By regularly stating these you enhance the process and your running.

- **Your targets and goals will change over time.** As they do, be sure to recreate them in writing, to keep them valid and powerful, and to keep yourself in action with them.

- **Set aside a specific "quiet" time to work on these components** in your *Magical Running Workbook* or journal. This very process of routine and discipline will bring rapid results, and provide your running with a unique and peaceful rhythm. As you bring your physical and now your mental powers to bear, you will experience a unique level of enjoyment and success in your running. By continuing with these principles, your sport will grow in stature as something that you love. It will become an integral part of your life.

- **Be flexible and kind to yourself when doing these creative exercises.** Often, when people realize that the way they have been viewing a certain aspect of their running is not the truth, but rather just one perspective, they become angry, frustrated or even embarrassed. This is not necessary. In fact the realization that a particular way in which you have been going about something (as if it is the only way), is but one of a number of alternatives, is called a *satori*, or a moment of instant awakening. Especially when you understand that the perspective that you had as the truth about your running is ineffectual or even destructive. This awareness that some "truth" is but a paradigm and that there are other choices that can be made is a great breakthrough.

The inability to see how your thinking stops you is typical of how we are. It is relatively easy to see where others are at fault, but our own errors are essentially invisible to us. One of the purposes of this book is to provide you with an approach by which you can exercise effective introspection and discover where and how ineffective mindsets hamper your running experience. If necessary forgive yourself for not immediately seeing the alternatives you have, and give yourself space to grow. Have fun with it all! After all, one of the primary reasons for running is to have fun, even at the very highest level.

- **Share your efforts with someone you trust.** Find a person who wishes to contribute to you. Someone who helps provide insight into your thoughts, wishes, desires, expectations and creations. Allow them to hold you responsible for the commitments you have made to yourself and your running. This simple act of sharing will multiply your efforts immensely and allow for breakthroughs of unexpected proportions. This phenomenon enhances your chances of success.

In most cases, runners tend to train at least in pairs, if not in larger groups, so finding a like-minded partner shouldn't be too difficult. Your responsibility toward another to whom you have committed your support usually greatly surpasses any commitment you might have to yourself. Such an agreement of mutual support leads to synergistic growth brought about by taking responsibility for supporting another's success.

- **There is no right or wrong way to do the exercises.** You have set in motion a process that will bring about healthy and effective growth in your running. The more you participate, the easier the exercises will become, until the process of introspection takes on a life of its own. People often work at their jobs because they feel they have to or are obliged to, and this is accepted behavior. Yet somehow in matters of self-realization, like running or marriage, one tends to shy away from "working at it." It's as if things should just work out. This is not the case, and by working on the mental side of your running you will gain so much more from it. In this way your running will become the way it was always meant to be – magical and fulfilling.

- **Realize that your enthusiasm will ebb and flow.** What you require from your running will change over time. Regularly revisit these pages and assess your relationship to running and what you desire from it in order to create the appropriate emphasis.

- **Evaluate your progress regularly.** At the end of each chapter you will find a weekly self-evaluation component. Additionally, at the end of the book, you will find an annual global summary for 13 monthly blocks. The process is simple: evaluate each week's efforts in each of the 12 key concepts on the provided 5-point scale. After four weeks, calculate your average and transfer this figure to the annual global summary at the back of the book. In this way you can plot your growth on a weekly, monthly and annual basis. The discipline required to commit to this process will cultivate the value and magic you will experience through the journaling activities.

Should you wish to continually create magical running for yourself, it is highly recommended that you use the *Magical Running Workbook* in conjunction with this book.

"A lot of athletes forget that, above all, the body is only the house of their spirit; the body will do what the mind tells it to do."

- TONI HASSLER (SWISS NATIONAL COACH)

Now to the adventure of new and exciting running!

AFFIRMED RUNNING
THE LANGUAGE OF SUCCESSFUL RUNNING

"What we tell ourselves can either help us or hurt us, depending on what the message is."
- JERRY LYNCH

Like visualization, affirmations are considered a major motivational tool by the world's elite athletes. Affirmations are phrases that remind you of who you need to be to deliver the performance you desire. Phrases such as the following bring about changes in your attitude that powerfully support your ability to perform:

"I enjoy my running. I am a winner. My fitness is excellent. I am great at what I do. I run exceptionally under pressure. I am an excited runner. I am a true leader. I can... I do..."

"During training sometimes, when the body lagged and the mind wandered,
I would bring myself back by shouting out aloud, 'Come on body;'
then I learned to shout that internally for racing purposes."

- PRISCILLA WELCH
LONDON AND NEW YORK MARATHON WINNER,
OLYMPIAN AND CANCER SURVIVOR

It is crucial that you take responsibility for what you say to yourself and others. If you say, "I don't think I'll run well today," then you will more than likely run poorly. You determine your actions with your self-talk, because you react to how you feel. Happily, that also means that if you say you run well, then your words begin the process of a good run.

The first step is to become aware of how you affirm against yourself dozens of times in a day. Statements like: "I can't do that. I'm so slow. I'm useless on the hills. I can't seem to find the time to train. I'll never beat Joe. I've no real talent. This sport is not for me. I'm tired," and so on are examples of how you affirm against yourself. If you recognize yourself in any of these statements, you've been the victim of your own defeating affirmations. Your memory of these experiences is probably enough to provide proof of the amazing power of affirmations—albeit negatively!

HOW WE SAY WE ARE, WE BECOME

Affirmations become self-fulfilled prophecies. You will fall into step with what you say and think of yourself as a runner. Sadly, people most often seem predisposed to negative affirmations. These are no truer than the positive ones, but just as powerful. Just as these self-destructive affirmations become reality, so too do the powerful, positive, uplifting and creative ones. You might as well use these!

Choose for yourself and not against. Say, "I am strong. I am fit. I am light. I am having fun. I am capable." These affirmations put into action the physical and mental processes of pre-programming both the conscious and the sub-conscious minds. If you recite them regularly, they will begin to serve you in the most pleasant ways, even when you are under pressure.

When you are physiologically tired this process becomes more challenging. You become irrational and your conscious mind can miss important cues and exaggerate others that are less important. For example, you might feel you are running powerfully. Suddenly you see a distance marker and the time on your stopwatch indicates that you are running more slowly than you thought. Immediately you interpret this negatively. You allow your powerful mindset to become sabotaged by an interpretation that is fraught with self-defeating consequences. You might not even consider that the marker could be wrong, or that you've made a miscalculation, or that the wind, weather or course may be affecting your time. Perhaps feeling powerful could be more meaningful to you than any objective measure of success.

When it comes to choosing what you believe, how you see something is how it is. That is why the "truth" of a situation is irrelevant when it comes to choosing how you will respond. You will respond according to your interpretation. This is why you should firstly be as open-minded and as objective as you can, and secondly interpret things that happen in such a way that you can make them work for you.

" All our knowledge has its origins in our perceptions."

- LEONARDO DA VINCI

Thinking through all possible scenarios before a run can help you avoid jumping to unsupported and unsubstantiated conclusions when you are tired. These negative thoughts can beat you up unnecessarily. When they occur, use an affirmation that says, "Judge your judgments." It is NOT the facts that hold you back, but your responses to them.

"I know that I am not seeing things as they are,
I am seeing things as I am."

- SUSAN HAYWARD

It is not possible to cover all bases, but it is possible to create and use affirmations that are entirely immune to arbitrary and out-of-context occurrences. For example, "I handle all and any situation." Instead of allowing challenging occurrences to derail your magnificent efforts, recognize them and affirm positively and creatively.

AFFIRMATIONS IN ACTION

One of the finest road-racers to come out of the United States, Jon Sinclair, reached a turning point in his career when he discovered the power of affirming himself repeatedly before a race:

"I've always liked cross-country racing, but have never been very good at it. When I was 22 years old I dedicated my whole fall racing season to preparing for the National Cross Country Championships and trained entirely on grass to get used to the surface. I struggled to get a comfortable 'feel,' but the training went well, and I arrived in Pocatello, Idaho, for the race feeling prepared, but unsure about racing on the soft ground.

"I spent the night before the race in a friend's basement on an air mattress and, needless to say, didn't sleep very well. It seemed like I woke up every hour anxiously looking at the clock waiting for morning. Each time I woke up I thought about the race and at some point started saying a mantra to myself, 'I can win.' By early morning the words became 'I will win.' I was repeating this phrase over and over again each time I drifted off to sleep. This must have occurred at least a dozen times.

"By the time I left that basement to go to the race location the words 'I can win' were constantly repeating in my head. In fact, I was starting to believe it in spite of my doubts about the soft, muddy surface, which has always been difficult for me.

"I did win the race and I am now convinced it would not have occurred unless I had happened on what has become a habit: repeating positive phrases before racing. Now, before racing I always try to say and think words that are positive in direction. It is not always 'I can win', but the thoughts and words are always in support of a goal ("target") I have decided is possible for the day. Starting 1-2 days before a race I choose 1 or 2 short phrases that I can repeat to myself. These phrases help to relieve nervousness and create a positive 'self-talk' that supports my efforts in the race."

HOW TO CONFIRM SUCCESS

- Speak affirmations in the present infinitive tense, as if they are occurring now and into the future. For example, "I train scientifically and reap the rewards."

- You DO NOT have to believe your affirmations for them to succeed powerfully: You simply have to say/do them (See Chapter 7).

- Affirmations are more effective when designed to be spoken rhythmically. For example, "I train to succeed, to run as I need." When in the midst of a run they serve as powerful mantras that keep you in the Zone (Chapter 8) and fully focused.

- Affirmations require regular and consistent repetition to be most effective. Do everything in your power to remind yourself to say these affirmations as often as is possible. Remember that for years your subconscious mind has been accidentally and automatically pre-programmed by many affirmations—some useful and many destructive. The only way to rid yourself of these damaging and self-sabotaging affirmations is to replace them with positive, powerful and self-inspiring ones. This takes time.

- Essentially there is no such thing as change—for the essence of that which you wish to change remains. You can only replace old ineffectual habits and thinking with new, effective methods. This requires constant drilling, repetition and practice. For example, "I perform beyond my training and obvious capabilities, because I believe this of myself and constantly remind myself of this."

- Your affirmations should be updated regularly. Affirmations that you have mastered you can discard. Regularly create new ones in writing. Put them up in places you are likely to see them most often, in varying colors, shapes and sizes. They should be constant reminders and therefore be moved around a great deal so that you always notice them. Ensure that they do not become "invisible" by remaining in the same place for too long.

- Share your affirmations with friends, loved ones and all who support you in your running endeavors. Teach them how to affirm, and support them with their affirmations. When you do this you reinforce your successful behavior. Affirmations assist you in staying responsible to the commitments that you have made. "I always give of my best" can be an affirmation at the forefront of your mind when those you care about and who know your commitment are present and supporting you. You honor the promises that you have made to others so much more easily than those you have made to yourself. Become known for your success in this regard.

- Say your affirmations out loud. This might be a little daunting for some of you in the beginning, but you literally alter the programming of your mind by doing this.

Of all of the means available to you to create a running life that is far beyond your logical comprehension and experiences, affirmations are at the forefront of manifesting this magic.

" I FEEL GREAT WHEN I RUN BECAUSE I SAY SO"
"I AM A CHAMPION, FOR I SAY SO"

DESIGNING YOUR OWN AFFIRMATIONS

IT IS RECOMMENDED THAT YOU FIRST BE CLEAR AND RELAXED BEFORE
THESE EXERCISES. (See Clearing, Relaxation and How to Relax in Chapter 7.)

Create affirmations for each component of your running life:

For an early morning run:

_____

_____

_____

EXAMPLES: *"I know how much I love running at dawn"*
"I love how I feel during the day when I've run in the morning"

Before a challenging run/session:

_____

_____

_____

EXAMPLES: *"In this session I grow immensely"*
"I love challenges and who I become through meeting them"

Before a race:

_____

_____

_____

EXAMPLES: *"I love to race"*
"I race well because I am prepared"

During a race:
    At the start:

_____

_____

_____

EXAMPLES: *"I start calmly and efficiently"*
"My excellent pace judgment sets up a perfect race"

At challenging points:

_____

_____

_____

EXAMPLES: *"I gain advantages through challenges, because I have a strategy"*
"I can handle anything"

Before and during hills:

_____

_____

_____

EXAMPLES: *"I float up hills using my strength and good form"*
"Hills draw me rapidly to the top"

Three-fourths of the way into the race (the "wall" zone):

_____

_____

_____

EXAMPLES: *"I focus intently on the job at hand"*
"My powers of concentration are a hallmark of my running"

Near the end:

_____

_____

_____

EXAMPLES: *"I begin my finishing kick early, because I am trained and
confident"*
"By holding my form and relaxing I ensure an excellent finish"

To get into the groove/zone:

_____

_____

_____

EXAMPLES: *"When I recall 'x' race, I instantly experience the same power and control"*
"By focusing only on each step, I enter my power zone, oblivious to those around me"

When "problems"/challenges arise:

_____

_____

_____

EXAMPLES: *"When I experience challenges, I become the solution"*
"I relish challenges for they are the ultimate opportunities for growth"
"I am tough"

Remember to recreate, add and choose 5-7 of your favorite affirmations to focus on each week.

AFFIRMATIONS CONFIRM SUCCESS TO YOURSELF.

FURTHER USEFUL HINTS & EXAMPLES

Continually play with your affirmations.

Highlight those you like best.

Record and keep quotes and pieces of inspirational writing.

Review them regularly (keep them in your *Magical Running Workbook* or journal).

Choose 5 to 7 new affirmations each week.

Create your own.

Say them aloud if possible (in the shower or car).

Place them where they can be seen regularly and keep putting up a fresh supply.

EXAMPLES OF AFFIRMATIONS:

"I strive for and claim the very best there is"

"There is plenty of success for all"

"I give myself permission to develop my full potential"

"I enjoy the bliss of fulfillment"

"All runners have their 'on' days-I welcome mine whenever they come"

"I am strong"

"I am smart about my training"

"I am dedicated and committed to doing the best I can"

"I am happy to be able to do what I do"

"I am experienced"

"Running rewards me"

"I am tough"

"I can handle anything"

"I am warm and loose"

"I enjoy the calm serenity I create for myself"

"I draw strength from the energy around me"

"I feel safe in the knowledge that I access ALL I have available on this journey"

"I apply my fitness evenly over the course of the run"

"I display my fitness with courage"

"I have power and strength beyond my conscious understanding"

"I draw on unseen powers"

"I am special"

"I am contributing to myself and others through this endeavor"

"I am ready for what God/the universe has to offer me"

"I am constantly improving"

"I continually achieve breakthroughs"

"I grow as a person and runner every day and every season"

"I am a great runner/racer"

"I accept assistance"

"I challenge myself"

"I already have all I need to perform as a winner"

"I feel triumphant and always compete like a champion"

"I am a winner—in all aspects of my life"

"There is greatness in my destiny"

"I am unique"

"I am EXTRA-ordinary"

"I challenge human limits"

"I believe in myself totally"

"I am fit"

"I am healthy"

"I am better than I have ever been before"

"My mind and actions support my well being in every way"

"I experience my immune system protecting me and growing stronger each day"

" I am grateful for my immune system which protects me from disease"

"I am a champion experiencing the challenges of the journey to the top"

"I am well"

"I do not need support, and yet I appreciate it"

"I gain by supporting and being supported"

"I am special beyond measure (to others and myself)"

"I am who I need to be to have what I desire"

"I do all that I need to do to be as successful as I dream to be"

"My dreams are grounded in reality"

"I am whole"

"I am balanced and very special"

"I am deserving"

"I am a winner"

"I lift above nerves, move beyond thinking it out, I just do it"

"I am uncluttered, uncomplicated, open and free to play"

"I am good enough"

"I am beautiful/handsome"

"I love what I do"

"I am loved"

"I am powerful"

"I am successful"

"I give more than I think I have"

"I can become whatever I visualize"

"I possess 'I can' power"

"I am very strong"

"I am exceedingly capable"

"I win races"

"I adapt to all conditions"

"I am world-class"

"I travel well"

"I have a strong constitution/immune system"

"I am relaxed under pressure"

"I am loved and respected"

"I am ready to take the opportunities given me"

"I am successful"

"I see opportunity in every situation"

"I am powerful"

"I am at peace when I run"

"Running serves me"

"I experience great joy when I run"

"I express love toward myself when I run"

"I express self-respect when I run"

HOW ARE YOU DOING WITH CHAPTER 2?
THE LANGUAGE OF SUCCESSFUL RUNNING

Record the date each time you focus on this component.

Date	Date	Date	Date

How do you rate your proficiency with this component?
(Write a date and a score out of five in the block next to the date.)

Rating Scale: 5 = excellent, 4 = good, 3 = acceptable, 2 = poor, 1 = very poor

Date	Score	Date	Score	Date	Score	Date	Score	4 week av.

Comments (Periodically write down any realizations you have in this area. How do preplanned affirmations effectively replace negative self-talk and ensure a self-fulfilling outcome that serves you?)

Date

Date

Date

THE START LINE
WHERE ARE YOU WITH YOUR RUNNING?

"We must not cease from exploration. And the end of all our exploring will be to arrive where we began and to know the place for the first time."
- T.S. ELIOT

As a coach to world-class athletes, runners seeking help to improve, approach me often. If I take them on, the first step of the journey to improve performance is to find out where they stand in their physical conditioning.

I am continually astounded that when asked to do a time-trial or other evaluation test to determine this, these athletes display real trepidation. They profess to not be fit enough or ready to take the test. Often they request a few weeks training to get ready!

I believe runners fail to progress as quickly as they might because they do not know where they are in their training. This is a common phenomenon. If you can keep hiding away from knowing where you stand, you can avoid taking responsibility for your true potential.

The primary step to progress is to accurately determine where you stand. In running that means accurate assessment of your physical fitness and your current mental state.

In order to move powerfully in a chosen direction with your running, you need to know exactly where you are.

HOLISTIC EVALUATION

The first step toward clearly knowing where you stand, requires a broad appraisal of your running and its context in your life. To determine this you can use the HASE (Holistic Actual Self Evaluation) questionnaire. This should be done on a weekly basis. It will serve as a constant reminder and reinforce the growing knowledge you have of yourself and how you function best.

It is important to realize that this evaluation involves only YOUR opinion regarding these specific areas of your running and life for any particular week. Such tests are counter-productive if runners use them to determine right or wrong. Use the evaluation only as an indicator of areas that require attention. A low score, for example, could help determine that your interpretation of how you regard a particular facet has a detrimental effect on your running.

SELF OPINION VS. THE OPINION OF OTHERS

Know that the opinions of those whom you trust and who care for you are bound to be more accurate and far less critical. Your opinion of yourself is often biased and overly harsh. It is therefore a good idea to share your self-evaluation with someone close to you (see Clearing in Chapter 7).

Realize that what you believe you can achieve, you are most likely to achieve. Similarly, you will not be able to achieve that which you do not believe is possible for you to do. Sadly in most cases, the opinion you have of yourself governs the outcome of your running far more powerfully than the facts of your ability. Consider too that the opinion others (like coaches and friends) have of your running is far more likely to be accurate. This is so because who you are as a runner is determined by how those around you perceive you to be. You might incorrectly believe that how you view yourself is how you really are. Listen to the opinion of others who are committed to you. Attempt to see yourself as they see you. Your running will flourish.

Lorraine Moller, the New Zealand runner who came 5th in the inaugural women's Olympic marathon in Los Angeles, labeled herself as "the best of the rest." For years she won every race she ran in if the "best" women weren't there. Finally, in a lesser and shorter race she came up against one of the women who had beaten her in that Olympics. She was running in second place to the Olympic medallist, when suddenly the woman indicated that she should pass her. Lorraine did this and ran on to victory. She'd shaken the self-defeating belief and went on to win a bronze medal in the Barcelona Olympic marathon 8 years after her first Olympics, despite being past her best physical years.

She'd also taken to heart the wise words of the great New Zealand coach Arthur Lydiard, who told her that very few athletes have a good run at the Olympics. She interpreted his words to mean that she was already one of the best and therefore only had a handful of girls to beat on the day. She did not even consider having a bad run as a possibility. At the start line she threw away her watch, saying to herself, "Someone'll take my time, but I've got a medal needs winning."

In summary, it is strongly recommended that when you evaluate yourself, you do so with strong consideration of how others who care about you and whom you love and trust see you.

DISCOVER SPECIFIC PROBLEM AREAS

The purpose of the exercise in this chapter is to identify "problem areas" and then to bring more sharply into focus any vague feelings you might have that something is not quite right in some area. Control in these areas comes from specifically identifying where your dissatisfaction comes from. Only then can you effectively act.

In this way the confusing and insistent "fears" that you might have about certain aspects of your running become clearly identified.

Once your fears are clarified in this way, it will be easier for you to see that:

- the "problem" is manageable
- you have choices that will lead to solutions

It is always easier to ask for assistance when you have first attempted to solve the situation yourself. Should a problem remain seemingly unsolvable, this exercise provides a starting point from which to take action. Specifically, speak to someone you trust who can provide insight and advice.

Remember that a problem can seldom be solved on the level that it was created. For example, should you realize that you always start your final sprint too soon, chances are that you do it because you don't have the patience or confidence to wait longer. You know this, but still do it. If however you tell someone and also have 2 or 3 people out on the course, a) to tell you to wait at the point you usually go and, b) to tell you to "go" when it's appropriate, the problem would more than likely be solved.

If you created a problem, chances are you need outside assistance to solve it.

HOLISTIC ACTUAL SELF EVALUATION (HASE)

HASE is designed to increase your awareness of all factors that affect your running. Everything you do in your life has an effect on everything else that you do, and taking responsibility around this insight provides an opportunity for incisive action and lasting change in these challenging areas. This incorporates the principal of holism, which states that all factors (in our lives) are relevant to performance in any specific area.

Date a column each week and evaluate yourself in the 15 areas suggested (see page 51). See if your score increases week by week. If so, you are being effective in addressing those issues that you have noticed require attention. By becoming aware of the specific nature of a situation, you improve your access to the responsibility and discipline required to effect lasting change.

OPERATIVE PRACTICES

It is strongly recommended that you note where (in which area) you rate yourself "2" or lower, and that you then create an operative practice for each point (see exercises at the end of the chapter). If you have no 2's, work on your 3's.

An operative practice is a new habit you design to replace an old ineffectual one. These old habits might have been created sub-consciously or automatically at some point to either protect you or allow you to "survive." They are now no longer effective. Replace them.

These operative practices should give you the ability to replace the behavioral pattern that brought about the low score. Continue consistently practicing the new way for 3 weeks—if you can keep this up for this period you should have established a new, more effective habit.

The secret is to notice the response that brings about the low score and to choose a new response. If a new habit does not take or stick, or is ineffective, replace it with yet another one and begin the 3-week process again, until you find resolution—even if it takes a year! See example on page 52.

A 5,000-meter runner I coach noticed she always said to herself before a race that she doesn't really have a kick. Whenever she caught herself saying this she would say out loud that when she raced no one would have a kick, because she would run them off their feet in the main part of the race. Within three races it began to work like a charm.

Don't try to change your habits, replace them with more effective ones.

As regards knowing where you are with your running: allow each time you test or evaluate yourself, each race, each run or session to objectively tell you where you are. Be aware of the interpretation or meaning you give to these results. Choose interpretations that help you. Deal only with the facts of your current running ability.

Don't dwell on the past and bemoan how your running has deteriorated. Saying, "If only I could run as I did when I was younger; if only I was fitter; if only I weren't injured; if only I had more time; if only I had a coach; if only I lived at altitude," is an exercise in futility and will eventually prove highly destructive. Such an approach will leave you feeling unfulfilled and helpless. It does not represent the present or the truth.

Dealing with the present and current situation provides access to improvement and control, and removes fear and unrealistic expectation. Work only with one week at a time and make sure it's the present week. This will help you to put the past where it belongs—in the past! In this way you can fully focus on the present. The present is the only thing you can do anything about anyway.

THE KEY TO SUCCESS LIES IN ACTION.

"WITH EACH RUN I AM AT THE BEGINNING OF A NEW JOURNEY"

DISCOVERING YOUR RUNNING GROUND ZERO
HASE (Holistic Actual Self Evaluation)

Rating scale: 5 = Excellent 4 = Good 3 = Acceptable 2 = Poor 1 = Very Poor

		WEEK	1	2	3	4
		DATES				
EVALUATION COMPONENTS						
1	Nutrition					
2	Sleep					
3	Recuperative activities					
4	Relationships					
5	Work / Occupation					
6	Time management					
7	Emotional / Social status					
8	Self discipline					
9	Holism					
10	Enjoyment					
11	Excellence (own standard)					
12	Performance (training & racing)					
13	Stress management					
14	Spiritual					
15	Mental					
	TOTAL					

NOTES:
3. Includes rest, extra sleep, massage, therapy, stretching/steam/sauna, whirlpool/jacuzzi, time off
7. Time out (socializing), community service, empathic behavior (listening and support), synergy (joint projects), intrinsic security
9. Do you regularly distinguish how other factors in your life affect your running?
11. How well are you faring according to your own standards?
12. How well do you rate yourself in comparison to other runners in the same environment as you?
13. Includes resolution "chat" sessions, handling/planning life details, relaxation drills, prioritizing
14. Includes value clarification and commitment, study and meditation/prayer
15. Includes specific reading, visualizing (and other mental skills), planning and writing

CREATING OPERATIVE PRACTICES

Note the areas in which you scored a 1, 2 or 3 and create the necessary operative practices to address them.

EXAMPLE: Component: *# 1   Nutrition*

I give myself a 2 for nutrition, because I feel I don't eat enough fresh fruit.

Operative practice:
I eat one piece of fresh fruit in the morning, take two pieces to work to eat during the day and take one to my workout session, so that I can eat it just after running. I buy sufficient fruit for this on a regular basis and consistently do this for three weeks, or until it becomes a healthy, effective, self-nurturing habit.

Component: # ....

Operative practice:

_____

_____

_____

Date Begun

Component: # ....

Operative practice:

_____

_____

_____

Date Begun

Component: # ....

Operative practice:

_____

_____

Date Begun [   ]

Component: # ....

Operative practice:

_____

_____

Date Begun [   ]

Component: # ....

Operative practice:

_____

_____

Date Begun [   ]

Component: # ....

Operative practice:

_____

_____

_____

Date Begun [   ]

Component: # ....

Operative practice:

_____

_____

_____

Date Begun [   ]

"The more deeply the path is etched, the more it is used,
the more it is used, the more deeply it is etched."

- JO COUDERT

ENSURING WHOLE RUNNING

To have whole and complete running, you need to have a whole life. This requires managing your own environment.

All aspects of your life are relevant to your running performance. By being aware of all the variables that contribute to performance, you can arrange them to best suit your running. These components strongly affect your immune system and your general well being. Addressing these proactively (in a planned, preventative manner) ensures consistent training and progressive predictable performance.

The following exercise is designed to give you a weekly global view of how your running is progressing. Use this framework to track the important variables in your running life.

WEEK STARTING:

	Am HR	Sleep	Pm Z's	Am Wgt	Msge	Joy	Fun	Space	Supp	Bad Occ	Meals
Mon											
Tues											
Wed											
Thur											
Fri											
Sat											
Sun											
Total											
Av.											

See key on page 57.

WEEK STARTING:

	Am HR	Sleep	Pm Z's	Am Wgt	Msge	Joy	Fun	Space	Supp	Bad Occ	Meals
Mon											
Tues											
Wed											
Thur											
Fri											
Sat											
Sun											
Total											
Av.											

WEEK STARTING:

	Am HR	Sleep	Pm Z's	Am Wgt	Msge	Joy	Fun	Space	Supp	Bad Occ	Meals
Mon											
Tues											
Wed											
Thur											
Fri											
Sat											
Sun											
Total											
Av.											

WEEK STARTING:

	Am HR	Sleep	Pm Z's	Am Wgt	Msge	Joy	Fun	Space	Supp	Bad Occ	Meals
Mon											
Tues											
Wed											
Thur											
Fri											
Sat											
Sun											
Total											
Av.											

KEY:

Am HR   Record your waking (resting) heart rate

Sleep   How many hours did you sleep this past night? (include 1/2 hours)

Pm Z's   How long was your afternoon nap (if you had one)?

Am Wgt   Weigh yourself on Fridays, after a trip to the bathroom and before any food/fluid

Msge   Record any massage or physical therapy sessions you had

Joy   Rate your day out of 5 in terms of enjoyment (1 being very poor, 5 being excellent)

Fun   Check to indicate whether you did a planned trip or activity for fun and relaxation

Space   Rate your day out of 5 as to whether you felt in control and at peace (1 being very poor, 5 being excellent)

Supp   Record whether you took any vitamin supplements

Bad Occ   Check whether you had a bad occurrence on a given day

Meals   Record the number of sit-down meals you had on a given day

LOOK AFTER THE DETAILS AND SUCCESS BECOMES A FORMALITY.

DEALING WITH SELF-DEFEATING RUNNING BELIEFS

As time goes by, you might notice that before you take on challenging runs certain negative occurrences from your past come to mind. Such thoughts can severely limit you, as they end up creating your belief system regarding specific areas.

For example, your thought that "I never run well when it's windy" came about as a result of some past occurrence. As time went by you gathered proof to support this self-defeating belief. Eventually it took on a life of its own and became your truth. Therefore when it is windy you powerfully and successfully decide you will do poorly and you manifest the negative result you are focusing on.

List these "stories" you have about yourself. Below each of these, in the space provided, create an affirmation (Chapter 2) that counters this paradigm. Promise yourself that each time you catch yourself entertaining this defeatist belief from your past, you will repeat your affirmation (out loud and repeatedly if possible). Then praise yourself for recognizing it.

EXAMPLE:

"Story":   *"I always run poorly at altitude."*
Affirmation: *"At altitude I go out conservatively and finish strongly."*

"Story":   _____

Affirmation: _____

_____

_____

"Story": _____

Affirmation: _____

_____

_____

"Story": _____

Affirmation: _____

_____

_____

"Story": _____

Affirmation: _____

_____

_____

"Story": _____

Affirmation: _____

_____

_____

FURTHER USEFUL HINTS & EXAMPLES

You cannot effectively advance when you fear how unprepared you might be. Knowing where you stand is an exercise in honesty that frees you up to face where and who you are. Then you can begin.

What is your real physical condition? Know this before you begin making predictions or assumptions. Accurately assess where you are in ALL departments. Determine what you really want and work from there when you assess yourself.

Social pressure and subsequently the ego might have you do or attempt things you are not ready for, nor would be willing to do were you allowed to truly decide for yourself. You are able to choose for yourself. Choose therefore on the basis of facts, not ego or wild assumption.

HOW ARE YOU DOING WITH CHAPTER 3?
WHERE ARE YOU WITH YOUR RUNNING?

Record the date each time you focus on this component

Date	Date	Date	Date

How do you rate your proficiency with this component?
(Write a date and a score out of five in the block next to the date.)

Rating Scale: 5 = excellent, 4 = good, 3 = acceptable, 2 = poor, 1 = very poor

Date	Score	Date	Score	Date	Score	Date	Score	4 week av.

Comments (Periodically write down any realizations you have in this area. How does the creation of an operative practice benefit your running?)

Date

Date

Date

SETTING RUNNING TARGETS
WHERE IS YOUR RUNNING TAKING YOU?

*"Ah, but a man's reach should
exceed his grasp or what's a heaven for?"*
- ROBERT BROWNING

Goals are an essential part of running success. Virtually every runner—from the beginner to the advanced competitor—has them. One runner's goal might be to set a new PR (personal record) in the 10K, while another's could be to run a certain number of miles/kilometers a week, and another's could be to complete a marathon.

Many runners use these goals to measure their success in the sport. They find satisfaction when they achieve their stated objectives.

Sounds reasonable, doesn't it? After all, isn't that what goals are there for—to measure success? Yes and no. In fact, in this chapter I'm going to ask you to re-think goals and your approach to them.

Runners who do not use goals in a healthy and productive manner find themselves continually frustrated in their careers. Even when they achieve a desired milestone, they cannot understand why they do not feel as fulfilled and happy as they thought they would be.

If they thought about it, they might realize that they were having the most fun, and experiencing the greatest degree of fulfillment while they were striving for their achievement—not after completing the act. In fact, the greater the challenge you set yourself to achieve these "goals", the greater the sense of satisfaction and achievement you will experience while on the journey.

Understanding how to properly set and use targets and goals is crucial to a happy and successful running career. It is of great importance to remind yourself of this while you are training, so that you can gain the full benefit and enjoyment of it while you are doing it! This will go a long way towards alleviating the sense of anti-climax you might feel if the sole measure of your endeavor was whether you achieved a specific performance or not.

TARGETS VS. GOALS

For the purposes of this program and for your ultimate fulfillment in running, it is very important that you differentiate between the creation of targets and goals. This difference between the two can be described as the difference between: "What we physically want" (targets) and, "Who or what we want to be" (goals).

Targets are measurable outcomes: race times, results, team selection, positions and other specific running achievements. The purpose of a target is to provide a focal point, and in that way targets determine your direction. They do not define the process.

It is easy to lose your way without targets, especially if matters are challenging and tough, or when you are tired. Targets therefore indicate direction and do not involve the how. Targets are like magnets that draw you along your chosen path. They are not the very things, that should you achieve them, would make your running complete. Rather, when you reach them, they provide you with satisfaction by indicating that you are on course with your training. You then simply set new targets out there in the future to draw you along for the next part of your journey.

Do however celebrate the achievement of targets; dwell on them, enjoy them and savor the sweetness of success. If you accept the achievement of targets as just another run, you risk losing your passion and drive. Let go of your defeats, remember your victories.

Goals, on the other hand, encompass the broader spectrum from emotion to attitude, that make you the person you are, and that keep you on course to reach your targets and more. While a target might be a sub-20 minute 5K, for example, a goal would be to learn lessons from every racing experience, no matter the outcome.

In most literature and in everyday language (as in the beginning of this chapter), therefore, the "goals" runners commonly refer to will become "targets" for the purposes of this text. That's not to say that the concept of goals as generally found in literature is incorrect. Rather, by separating the concepts, this program provides greater access to the actions and process required to achieve both goals and targets; this occurs by distinguishing between "what" you want and "who" you want to be. Making the distinction between targets and goals will allow you to add dimension and clarity to your progress, and ultimately afford you greater access to the elements that bring about fulfillment.

Read the following quote by motivational guru Anthony Robbins:

"Goals are a means to an end, not the ultimate purpose of our lives. They are simply a tool to concentrate our focus and move us in a direction. The only reason we pursue goals is to cause ourselves to expand and grow. Achieving goals by themselves will never make us happy in the long term; it's who you become, as you overcome the obstacles necessary to achieve your goals, that can give you the deepest and most long-lasting sense of fulfillment."

Now reread the above quote replacing the word "goals" with "targets". That is the manner in which we mean for targets to be addressed.

To view targets as goals in your running is to seriously limit yourself and ultimately set yourself up for failure, and a lifetime of hollow and empty achievements.

The rest of this chapter will focus on targets and how to set the appropriate ones for your individual needs. Chapter 5 will address setting goals.

IT'S THE PROCESS THAT COUNTS

To fully enjoy the process requires that you be present in the "now" of each running moment. The fulfilled runner is one who enjoys the training and racing experience equally. They consider both activities as having their own value, and they do not train in order to race—they train to train, and race to race.

By visualizing an upcoming race or training session (Chapter 7), you are mentally reviewing it. This greatly helps you to remain in the moment. Plan enough time for each workout to further ensure that you remain fully present to your running and don't have to rush through the experience.

Ultimately, you have little control over your journey's outcomes and results. Therefore, once you have set your targets it is crucial that you detach or remove yourself from them, as the value of setting targets lies in the process they draw you through. If you only have targets, you are left with a feeling of emptiness and failure if they are not achieved. This "all-or-nothing" approach leads to the experience that you have no control over your running. Wind, weather, hills, inaccurate courses, and any number of circumstances can conspire to unravel your carefully made plans regarding your targets. Unlike goals, where you can choose a behavior, no matter what the circumstances, when you set a target, you might not achieve it for various reasons.

For example, if you choose to be brave (your goal), you can be, no matter what the circumstances. On the other hand, if your target is to run a certain time in a race or on a training run, and a herd of cattle unexpectedly crosses the road in front of you, you will be unable to achieve your target, despite your best intentions.

DETACH FROM YOUR TARGETS, FOCUS ON ACTIONS

Therefore you should quickly learn to detach your expectations from target outcomes. Do this by reviewing what your targets are, and then focusing on the actions that you have to execute to achieve them. The mind is like a TV screen, it can hold only one image "up on screen" at a time. Letting go of an attachment means that it is not at the forefront of your mind when you are running. This should in no way diminish your commitment to achieving your targets, but rather it relieves you of the need for concern in an area where you have limited influence. (Unless of course you can change things like the weather or can effectively communicate with cows!)

SETTING TARGETS

Ill chosen targets may limit you. When you underestimate yourself and/or your ability, you may end up reaching your targets too easily. While initially this might sound great (instant success!), you actually run the risk of limiting both your performance and your satisfaction. You are also more likely to settle for less than you are capable of.

Some runners also suffer from a self-defeating response when faced with actually achieving their objectives. That's because they have been programmed to doubt themselves: When finally faced with success they will tend to sabotage the effort through lack of self-confidence. Think about a race where you were right on your hoped-for pace, and it even felt easy. Was your reaction one of quiet confidence? Or rather of panic that you'd never be able to keep it up? Self-doubters will respond like this: "Oh my goodness, I'm getting close to my target, I must be tired now. This is going to be very hard." If that sounds like you, then you are not allowing your body to show you its limits, but rather allowing your doubting mind to run matters. Do not let your mind sabotage your success as you approach your targets.

TARGETS MUST SERVE YOUR PURPOSE, AND NOT HOLD YOU BACK. THEY MUST CREATE AWARENESS. THEY MUST BE REALISTIC, BUT YOUR AIM MUST BE UNREASONABLY HIGH!

UNREASONALBLE TARGETS

The term "unreasonably" is used so that you can also choose targets beyond your current level of (reasonable) thinking. Consider that what you believe you can reasonably achieve at any given phase of your running career is valid as a short-term target. However, by setting long-term targets you create a structure, or a time-line upon which you can place your short-term targets in context, as you step into the unknown.

Being reasonable has cost many runners dearly. The tough British runner, Priscilla Welch, who started running only in her mid thirties, learnt this lesson the hard way in the only Olympics she ever competed in. Her refusal, in her own mind, to consider winning as an option brought her 5th place.

"I remember David (her husband) saying, we were going for a medal, and I recall thinking that was 'pie in the sky', and agreed to focus on the bronze —Dave was focusing on the gold. Arthur Lydiard always said that only 20% are shooting for medals in the field, the rest are just content to be there. How very right he was. I was in 5th place until Lorraine Moller overtook me, so I guess David wasn't too far out. Had I had more experience and self-confidence, maybe I would have reacted like Joanie (Benoit-Samuelson) did. She made the right decision at the right time in a marathon that was dictated by doing well, because it was the first in an Olympics (Los Angeles, 1984), and everyone was looking at everyone else until Joanie went —I remember thinking: 'Goodness me I'm still with them', but never did I think about taking them on, I was very much a rookie and in awe of names."

You should however base your targets in reality, not fantasy. If, for example, you are an adult 50-minute 10K runner, who has been running consistently for 8 years and utilizing an advanced training program successfully, it would be "unrealistically" achievable to be aiming at a sub 45-minute performance. Even a sub 40-minute run could fire up your imagination! But to dream of being an Olympic trialist at 10,000-meters would not create any magic in your training or performances. The discrepancy would be too great, and that part of your mind that accepts such seeds of possibility would not absorb or accept this.

Those that do harbor ludicrous expectations suffer from delusions of grandeur that can only ultimately hurt them and those around them. This is especially true where the physical realities of measurable ability are obvious; strongly built 200-pounders do not win marathons, but they can have the mindset of a running champion and perform beyond what can reasonably be expected, as a result of powerful target setting. To test for this you need to search for a deep sense of trust and conviction. You will know you can, even if you have no idea how.

Peter Maher, the Canadian Olympian, started his career as a distinctly obese (200-pounds plus) jogger, who walk-jogged to lose weight! He was to remain a tall, larger runner, but became an inspiration to many runners as he ran from the ranks of the 4-hour marathoner to the sub 2:15 elite.

Successful author and accomplished Olympic marathoner, Don Kardong warns against only having long-term targets, based on misguided beliefs. He wisely suggests setting targets within your current framework. He states: "this reminds me of high school runners who tell me they want to run in the Olympics. I try to convince them to aim for one thing at a time, based on where they are in life.

If they're a high school senior, try to be the best senior they can. My own Olympic dream only took shape after continued successes at lower level targets."

Later in this chapter you'll be setting out both short-and long-term targets. By setting numerous targets that are to be achieved at different times you are more likely to stay directed over the course of your program. For example, if you are a beginning runner and your only target was to eventually run a marathon, you would likely feel adrift for years without knowing how well you were progressing toward that target. Instead, you'll want to think in terms of the short-term, a period of one season to one year, and the long-term, a period from two years up to a lifetime. Then you can set a target of completing a 10K this summer, a half-marathon next summer, and a marathon over the course of the next three years. Similarly you can set mileage and training targets over time. For example, you might want to be doing 30 miles (50 kilometers) per week come January 1st and build by adding 5 miles (8 kilometers) per week until you reach 50 miles (80 kilometers) per week. You might also set a target of doing formal track work once a week come the spring, as an example.

Knowing where you are going does not necessarily imply having the details worked out in full. It is more a case of being sure of your commitment to excellence. Clear focus on targets ensures that you have a success mentality and are not looking for excuses at every barrier you encounter. If you set targets just beyond your current reach, they ensure that you are always actively striving. This is in direct contrast to being easily put off your course because you are never actually clear about what you are aiming to achieve.

SET YOUR OWN TARGETS

Targets should not become burdens, but rather a guiding light to your running. Be sure you are setting targets that are appropriate for you, and not for somebody else. To help you aim and plan your journey of joy and excellence in running, you should constantly ask yourself the following questions:

- What excites me about my running?
- What am I reaching for with my running?
- What inspires me about running?

In this way you can firmly establish a framework within which you can achieve all you set out to do with great joy, and discover a purpose and value in your running that is wildly beyond your expectations.

Never cease from:

- Wishing for and dreaming of all you desire.

- Asking for what you really want. Do this on all levels—in prayer or pondering, or in meditation, as well as on the physical level of making requests of friends, family and loved ones. Ask experts too: like coaches, therapists and people with unique expertise.

- Spending times of intense focus upon your running desires. Concentrate wholly during physical workouts and "mental workouts." Tight focus during running activities followed by complete breaks in which we don't even think about running, ensures the greatest and most specific focus.

- Always be passionate! Everything is empty without passion—pursuing running excellence in whatever form we choose is doomed to failure without passion. This is true with the whole of life. Train with passion. Share your running with passion. The depth of experience you will gain from a running life filled with passion greatly supercedes any level of running you might have previously experienced.

CONSIDER EACH TARGET ACHIEVED AS A MILESTONE
ON THE JOURNEY OF SUCCESS.

"I KNOW WHERE I AM HEADED WITH MY RUNNING"

DESIGNING YOUR TARGETS

Arrange your targets hierarchically, from those of highest importance (the long-term ones and those which seem the most difficult to achieve), to those that are soonest to be realized, the short-term targets.

Arrange your lifetime targets and your current event targets in the spaces provided. Examples appear at the end of the list to guide and inspire you.

LIFETIME TARGETS
LONG-TERM

1. _____

2. _____

3. _____

4. _____

5. _____

6. _____

7. _____

EXAMPLES:

- *To be a lifetime runner*
- *To win an Olympic Medal*
- *To break "x" minutes for 10K*
- *To run a marathon*
- *To run 60 miles in a week*

CURRENT EVENT TARGETS
SHORT-TERM

1. _____
2. _____
3. _____
4. _____
5. _____
6. _____
7. _____

EXAMPLES:

- *To place in the top 10 in "x" road race*
- *To run "y" time in this event*
- *To beat "so-and-so" on Saturday*
- *To run a PR*
- *To place in the top half of "this" event's field*

"MY RUNNING TARGETS DRAW ME LIKE POWERFUL MAGNETS THROUGH FULFILLING PERIODS OF TRAINING AND RACING"

FURTHER USEFUL HINTS & EXAMPLES

Draw up a list of your targets.

Regularly review this list and add to it.

Check your targets as you achieve them and leave them on the list as visible proof of your progress.

Remember to arrange whatever targets you choose hierarchically, from the hardest to the easiest. You can have as many as you please. The more targets you have the greater the degrees of fulfillment, and the easier the steps to each next objective.

EXAMPLES:

- *To run a personal best*
- *To win a specific race*
- *To run under a specific time*
- *To complete a specific event without walking*
- *To have this race be one where all your plans come together*
- *To break/set a record*
- *To achieve a specific position (e.g. top 3 places or top half of the field, or a specific age group position)*

HOW ARE YOU DOING WITH CHAPTER 4?
WHERE IS YOUR RUNNING TAKING YOU?

Record the date each time you focus on this component

Date	Date	Date	Date

How do you rate your proficiency with this component?
(Write a date and a score out of five in the block next to the date.)

Rating Scale: 5 = excellent, 4 = good, 3 = acceptable, 2 = poor, 1 = very poor

Date	Score	Date	Score	Date	Score	Date	Score	4 week av.

Comments (Periodically write down any realizations you have in this area, or comment on how setting targets is assisting you with your running. Are you setting targets and regularly reviewing and relating to your running in terms of these targets? Is this process helping your running? Are you achieving your targets?)

Date

Date

Date

RUNNING GOALS
BEING THE PERSON YOU DESIRE

*"Great dancers are not great because of their technique:
they are great because of their passion."*
- MARTHA GRAHAM

FINDING THE HOLY GRAIL

Once you have arranged your targets (Chapter 4) hierarchically you can begin with goal setting. Targets determine the direction you are going to take, while goals represent the characteristics required to achieve those targets.

For a knight to discover the Holy Grail he must first be courageous, noble, faithful and pure of heart. The Holy Grail is the target, while the traits are the goals that must constantly be displayed to achieve the target. There is no failure in not discovering the grail, for what has been gained are the wonderful traits of faith, nobility, courage and purity. The purpose of the journey is the quest itself.

DETACH FROM OUTCOMES

Remember to keep your targets in your sights, but do not become attached to them. Your attention and focus are on the constant creation and recreation of your daily (and even hourly) goals. During a run, your targets are in the back of your mind, guiding your commitment. What must be in the foreground is your strength of purpose to execute the processes of success with discipline, joy and whatever other goals you deem necessary to achieve success.

Goals are those characteristics that you, as a runner need to display and become, to remain on course to reach your targets.

THE CHARACTERISTICS OF A SUCCESSFUL RUNNER

Spend some time determining what you believe the characteristics are that you require to achieve your targets. For example, "To run as I want to, I require of myself to exhibit the following characteristics in training, races and in my daily life:

- being patient
- believing in myself and my abilities
- believing I am a successful runner
- enjoying my running and participation in races
- asserting myself
- staying calm and relaxed
- knowing I have choices in any given situation"

See "FURTHER USEFUL HINTS & EXAMPLES" at the end of the chapter for more examples.

REFER CONSTANTLY TO YOUR GOALS

Your goals should always be with you. Carry them around with you, in your mind and literally. Paste them up in your room. Keep a list in your sports or gym bag and wallet. Remind yourself of them during your runs.

After each training run or race, ask yourself how you fared with regard to your goals. For example, "Was I patient out on the road today?"

Goals are easy to evaluate. For example, when you have not achieved a target that you set for yourself in a race, you can draw more value and satisfaction from determining how you measured up to your goals. After all, this is where you do have control.

Boston marathon winner Jacqueline Gareau is a petite and gracious marathon runner from Canada who played a major role in women's marathoning during the years leading up to the inaugural Olympic women's marathon in Los Angeles in 1984. She considers her breakthrough to have come at the 1984 Los Angeles marathon which she used as a build up race to the Olympics. After recording her best time in the '83 Boston marathon, she went on to finish 5th in the world championships in Helsinki. In that race, she lost concentration at a watering table and fell behind the lead bunch.

As a result Jacqueline resolved to work on the mental portion of her running. "I decided to really train myself to stay focused till the very end, (see Chapter 9). So by visualizing during each of my hard workouts, (see Chapter 7), how I would feel, using the key words regularly: *focus, relax* (see Chapter 8).

"At the start of this marathon, (Los Angeles), I felt very sharp and confident. I had a very positive attitude (see Chapter 2), I just felt light and powerful (Chapter 8). I couldn't wait to get going. I had been waiting so long for the opportunity to prove to myself that all the specific training I'd done would pay off. I was neck and neck with one competitor till the last 2 kilometers, then I decided to push the pace, three times trying to break away. The last time, it worked! She let me go and I finished strong and confident, like I had been at the end of my hard workouts. It really worked, so it was exhilarating, I felt so happy about this outcome since it came with great physical and psychological preparation. The satisfaction of work well done was so palpable, it'll always be in my mind."

In her own words Jacqueline so clearly shows how she focused on how she was to be, as opposed to what she had to do, and then achieved the target, which was to win the race.

DETERMINE THE PROCESSES OF SUCCESS

When you set goals, you are shaping the processes of success. That means deciding what characteristics, like commitment and dedication, you need in order to reach your targets. You and the other important people in your life will remember who you have become through your running, rather than what you have achieved. The characteristics that you consistently strive for are your goal traits. These traits keep you continually on the path of successful running.

This path will be sign-posted by the exciting targets you achieve along the way.

Priscilla Welch speaks of how much more she grew as a person through the goals she achieved in her running:

"You must first understand that I did not know that I had a talent for running. I was introduced to running aged 35 years, and purely for health (reasons).

"I was raised with negativity in England. Meeting David and being introduced to the sport of running for health, I found I was being educated into a positive thinker as well. At last I had found something I was good at—and I was loving it, and the freedom of thought it was giving me, along with confidence in actions."

Priscilla has won many races and, as a survivor of breast cancer, is a spokesperson for The Race for the Cure, a magnificent series of events that bears the standard for all who have suffered through this challenging disease.

CHOOSE TO BE A SUCCESSFUL RUNNER

Synthesizing this chapter and incorporating it as a part of your life requires that you honestly answer the following:

- — What characteristics define you as a runner?
- — What shows that you have what it takes to achieve what you set out to do?

Measure your success as a runner by how often you successfully display the characteristics (goals) you have chosen.

When you focus on "who" you are in races and achieve success this way, you will know that this approach works! Soon others will notice a change in your attitude (way of being as a runner) and the resultant success and enjoyment you experience in your running.

"We are what we repeatedly do.
Excellence, then, is not an act, but a habit."

- ARISTOTLE

"I KNOW WHICH HABITS TO DISPLAY DAILY TO ACHIEVE SUCCESS"

DETERMINING YOUR RUNNING GOALS

Write your goals in groups of seven. Have a new set each week. (These can be the same, but reword them and change their order.) Read them every morning, before each run, and last thing before you go to bed at night.

At the end of each run and race ask yourself if you were being the runner you set yourself to be in your goals. During training and racing remind yourself of your goals, for example, "Am I being patient?; Are my actions displaying my commitment?; Am I enjoying myself?"

My goal processes for week .... to .... are:

1. _____

2. _____

3. _____

4. _____

5. _____

6. _____

7. _____

EXAMPLE: *"I am a runner who finds joy in every run"*

See "FURTHER USEFUL HINTS & EXAMPLES" at the end of this chapter for other examples.

My goal processes for week .... to .... are:

1. _____
2. _____
3. _____
4. _____
5. _____
6. _____
7. _____

EXAMPLE: *"I am an assertive racer"*

My goal processes for week .... to .... are:

1. _____
2. _____
3. _____
4. _____
5. _____
6. _____
7. _____

EXAMPLE: *"I relish the challenges of running"*

My goal processes for week .... to .... are:

1. _____

2. _____

3. _____

4. _____

5. _____

6. _____

7. _____

EXAMPLE: *"During and after each run, I am fully aware of and appreciate the privilege that it is to run"*

"BY HONORING THE GOALS OF WHO I WANT TO BE AS A RUNNER, I BECOME THE PERSON WHO HAS THE LIFE I DESIRE. BY CONTINUALLY PLAYING THE ROLE OF MY DREAM RUNNER, I BECOME THE RUNNER I DESIRE."

I **DO** CREATE MY OWN DESTINY.

FURTHER USEFUL HINTS & EXAMPLES

Remember goals are processes that indicate who you want to be as a runner.

What kind of runner do you want to be to succeed at the level you desire?

What traits do you want to display as a runner?

What characteristics do you need to succeed?

EXAMPLES OF GOALS:

- *To be patient*
- *To have faith in myself and my ability*
- *To consistently believe I'm a winner*
- *To remain balanced throughout my training*
- *To have fun along the way and in the event itself*
- *To be assertive*
- *To be serene, calm and relaxed*
- *To remain in the moment each step of the way, and to "see" the past as irrelevant to the present*
- *To consistently know that each moment of running is my life and I choose it*
- *To always choose control of my destiny in each event*
- *To regularly and powerfully affirm myself*
- *To visualize success consistently throughout my preparation and the race itself*
- *To constantly refer to my mission in this period/for this race*
- *To be open to new approaches*
- *To allow my physical potential to shine through*
- *To love what I do. To love running. To love myself*
- *To seek and take opportunities to contribute through my sport*
- *To choose to increase my influence and reduce my concerns*
- *To instantly recognize problems as challenges that provide me with opportunities and to grasp these opportunities and run with them*

- *To know always that through my approach, I do my best and am completely satisfied after each effort*
- *To enjoy my training*
- *To get to races relaxed*
- *To allow the race to develop*
- *To keep it simple*
- *To be patient*
- *To draw strength from other runners and the crowd*
- *To be pulled along by fields of runners around me*
- *To be relaxed and efficient*
- *To use my strength from good training and have a positive mindset at the end of the race*
- *To use my strong mind in the last part of the race*

EXAMPLES OF AFFIRMATIONS:

- *"I am appreciative of my health and fitness"*
- *"I am confident of my fitness"*
- *"I am tough through having dealt with the discomfort of training and my experience"*
- *"I am committed to the effort a PR (personal record) requires"*
- *"I am optimistic and excited about this event"*
- *"I am excited at the opportunity"*
- *"I am focused on getting the job done"*

HOW ARE YOU DOING WITH CHAPTER 5?
BEING THE PERSON YOU DESIRE

Record the date each time you focus on this component

Date	Date	Date	Date

How do you rate your proficiency with this component?
(Write a date and a score out of five in the block next to the date.)

Rating Scale: 5 = excellent, 4 = good, 3 = acceptable, 2 = poor, 1 = very poor

Date	Score	Date	Score	Date	Score	Date	Score	4 week av.

Comments (Periodically write down any realizations you have in this area. How does focusing on what or who you need to BE help you achieve running success and satisfaction?)

Date

_____

Date

_____

Date

_____

A RUNNING MISSION
CREATING MEMORABLE RUNNING

"If you built castles in the air, your work need not be lost: that is where they should be. Now put the foundations under them."
- HENRY DAVID THOREAU

WHAT IS YOUR RUNNING LEGACY?

Steven Covey, renowned author and speaker on personal effectiveness, speaks of the purpose of life as being "to live, to love, and to leave a legacy." The power with which you live your life and the intensity of purpose you bring to your running is magically accelerated when you consider your efforts in the light of the legacy you wish to leave.

There is much to be learned from individuals who have experienced great success. One of the common denominators throughout the ages has been the dreams of greatness that these individuals have carried with them throughout their lives. Many of these great people have had a sense of history about them. They have stood firm when the only thing that kept them going was that one day they would be remembered for the choices they made and the actions they took.

The purpose of this chapter is to guide you in the application of your dreams. But first you must have dreams.

WITHOUT DREAMS THERE IS NOTHING

Back in the early 1980's, as a young high school coach, I dreamed of one day coaching an Olympic athlete. It did not matter that my young athletes were not even regional champions, nor did it matter that I lived in a country where the government policies were so inhumane that I could never hope to coach an athlete to international fame. South Africans were not allowed in international competition. All that mattered was that I had a dream, first as a schoolboy out running alone, battling Frank Shorter and Lasse Viren (my childhood Olympic heroes) in my imagination, and then later as a coach, striving to turn young excited runners into champions. This dream was first fueled by the encouragement of my loving and supportive parents, later by teachers and wise generous coaches who taught me my trade. Through various challenges, personal setbacks and politics, the dream always remained as the one golden thread that ran through it all.

Now there have been many successes, many victories. I will never forget the day in 1996 when with tears and joyous emotion I watched a brave, powerful, battle-scared little N'debele (a South African tribe) man, whom I had had the privilege to work with for four years prior to this event, run into that Olympic stadium in Atlanta and win the gold medal for himself, his newly liberated country and his beloved president, Nelson Mandela.

Yet still the dream remains. There are other athletes, other challenges and other races.

What are your dreams? What running legacy do you want to leave behind? What do you want people to remember about how you ran? How do YOU want to be remembered as a runner?

The answers to these questions will challenge you to create and execute the actions, runs and lifestyle that will lead to you being remembered as your dreams dictate.

To create a blueprint for your running life requires a mission statement. This is your personal philosophy that states how you want to be and what you want to do with your running. It is based on your unique values.

A powerful and effective mission statement is one that is created in your imagination as if you already are being the person you continually strive to be. In other words, your actions reflect a continuation of the process of being the person you wish to be remembered as. For example, "I am remembered as a runner who always gives of his/her best."

CREATING INDIVIDUAL RUNS

Before each run or race, imagine in clear detail that you are in conversation with a friend after the event. In this conversation, you explain how the run went. Ensure that the scenario you create is as you would want it. Place your emphasis on how it felt and what your emotional state was.

For example, "I really felt great in the race, everything just fell into place. My feel and ability to create the run were as never before. I ran like I've always believed I could run. What a joy! I loved every moment of it."

Note there is no mention of a result, time or outcome (see Chapters 4 and 5). The most effective way to come up with a scenario of this nature is to ask yourself the question: "How do I want to feel before, during and after this race?"

CREATING A LIFETIME RUNNING MISSION

It is also extremely useful to create a lifetime mission for your running. Imagine that it is 4 years from now. You are at your own funeral and 4 people are to speak about your life: a close family member, a friend, a fellow runner and someone who was your mentor. What do you want them to say about how you lived your life?

Then arrange your life, the living of it and your running in such a way that, when you do die, these things will be said about you. By traveling into the distant future in your imagination and looking back upon the nearer future, it becomes easier to realize how it is you want your running to be.

Once you have "seen" how you want your running career to be, it makes it far easier to take responsibility for the day-to-day actions of your running and racing. You should now have a very clear picture of where you are headed. Your commitment remains firm by having that legacy to live up to daily.

How would you like to be remembered? Here is an example:

"Susan was my favorite running partner, she was an inspiration to run with. She was tough and never quit. She always had time for all her friends. She taught me the value of patience and consistent training. She really loved her running. Her enjoyment was infectious. Every run with her was filled with miracles. Her racing philosophy was one I now live by: Run hard, keep it simple, no regrets and enjoy every single step—always!"

Much of how humans operate is determined by how we wish to be seen by others. As with affirmations, most people act this way unconsciously. Why not then increase the value and remove the negative by consciously deciding what it is you want to be remembered for? Whether you succeed or fail will be largely predetermined by your thinking prior to your actions. Your attitude, more than your ability, is the major determinant when it comes to choosing a course of action and how successful it will be.

It is not "facts" that determine the outcome of human endeavor, but the thinking of the people involved.

In the buildup to that first Olympic women's marathon in 1984 in Los Angeles, every woman who had world-class marathon running ability at the time was vying for gold in a race that was to become pivotal in how the world viewed woman's running.

Joan Benoit-Samuelson, who just weeks before the race had had surgery to her knee, reveals that her attitude played a huge role in her epic victory on that historic day. "I knew no one had trained as hard as I had. I have always been hard-working and passionate in all that I do." She goes on to say, "I could never not compete, even if it was at a different level. Running will always be a big part of my life with differing degrees of importance."

She won the race due in part to her amazing physical ability, honed to a fine edge through hard training, but in the end it came down to her thinking. "I always ran my own race. I never worried about the rest of the field," she says. "I just worked as hard as I could. I entered the Olympic marathon concerning myself with the race I would run, and not the race my competitors would run." In a race where the world's best were battling for the greatest running prize of all, she ran away with it.

A predetermined attitude prevailed, and she was handsomely rewarded for her courage.

DESIGNING A RUNNING MISSION

Create each race and important training runs in the spaces provided. You can use the example provided in the text. Use phrases like "How I felt was...; I said to myself...; I experienced...," and any other examples that indicate your internal state or decisions.

Do this regularly before events. Make sure you do it for the first time at least 48 hours before the event (longer before is preferable):

_____

_____

_____

_____

_____

_____

_____

_____

_____

_____

_____

See "FURTHER USEFUL HINTS & EXAMPLES" at the end of this chapter for an example.

LIFETIME RUNNING MISSION

Your lifetime running mission is something that will grow over the years and takes time to develop. Work on it regularly and adapt it as you progress as a runner. Write this all-important mission statement as if someone close to you and your running is writing it. Use the "Susan" example from the previous text pages to guide your efforts if need be.

How I remember .... (your name) as a runner is:

_____

_____

_____

_____

_____

_____

_____

_____

_____

_____

_____

FURTHER USEFUL HINTS & EXAMPLES

EXAMPLE OF A MISSION STATEMENT FOR A SPECIFIC EVENT:

"For this race I keep things simple and race harder than ever before. I keep my own perceptions out of the way. I am utterly victorious despite the outcome, for I am clear that the process is the race. I allow thoughts to rise and dissipate harmlessly and I honor my commitment to excellence. I give my all without judging myself. I experience total satisfaction and joy at having chosen to execute each step of the process powerfully. I trust myself and my fitness. This race is the stage upon which I give clear, full, uncluttered and total expression of myself as a runner and a human being."

EXAMPLE OF LIFETIME RUNNING MISSION STATEMENT:

"My running is a total physical expression of my humanity. When I run I am happy, free and fulfilled. Each run magnifies and multiplies these feelings. Running plays a major part in me being self-realized."

HOW ARE YOU DOING WITH CHAPTER 6?
CREATING MEMORABLE RUNNING

Record the date each time you focus on this component

Date	Date	Date	Date

How do you rate your proficiency with this component?
(Write a date and a score out of five in the block next to the date.)

Rating Scale: 5 = excellent, 4 = good, 3 = acceptable, 2 = poor, 1 = very poor

Date	Score	Date	Score	Date	Score	Date	Score	4 week av.

Comments (Periodically write down any realizations you have in this area. How does imagining each race before it is run, benefit your running? Similarly, how does knowing what and who you want to be remembered as in your running assist you in being responsible for each training run and race?)

Date
_____

_____

Date
_____

_____

Date
_____

_____

VISUALIZED RUNNING
SEEING YOURSELF RUN AND RACE SUCCESSFULLY

"Don't worry about Friday's race,
I've seen the movie – I stick with her
till 300-meters to go and then out-kick her for the win."
- LINDSAY HATZ
(ONE WEEK BEFORE WINNING THE GOLD MEDAL IN THE
1999 WORLD VETERAN GAMES 5,000-METER WALK)

The world's greatest athletes consider visualization the number one technique to ensure peak performance. The concept is simple. "See" how you achieve dream levels of running by imagining the performance through the use of all your senses. By seeing and feeling your performance ahead of time, you train your mind and body for success in actual running situations.

Professional runners fully utilize the power of this technique, and so can you.

"Visualization played an important part in my training and psychological build-up for my victories in the (South African) Comrades marathon" says Bruce Fordyce, former 50-mile world record holder, and 9-time winner of the world's most prestigious ultra marathon, the Comrades marathon (56 miles/90 kilometers).

"The process was both simple and informal. I did not set aside time to mentally rehearse success. It just used to happen—as long as certain ingredients were right. It was important, first of all, to know that I was truly fit—there could be no purpose in rehearsing for success if my body was not really fit. Race day also had to be close at hand, beckoning to me in an exciting and frightening way. It would have to be a long winter's evening run with dead leaves blowing in cold dark streets. The route would have to be very familiar to me so that there were no distractions. Running steadily and easily, my mind would then be free to wander. Suddenly I would find myself on the Comrades marathon course, on race day, at the front of the field on a key section of the course.

"So, two weeks before race day in 1986, I saw myself on 45th Cutting (a long steep hill 5 miles/8 kilometers from the finish). I planned to strike there and get away from any pursuers. In my mind I pictured, heard and smelt the car exhaust fumes, the crusty sweat on my cheeks, sore stiff legs. I could hear the hysterical yelling from the crowds lining the narrow corridor that remained for the runners. I could see the motorcycle escort just ahead of me. I visualized what was required. What I imagined was an almost imperceptible but smooth increase in pace, the faltering of my pursuers and the gradual realization that I had stretched, and then snapped the umbilical chord between myself and the rest of the field. I practiced keeping my temper in control when a spectator leaped in front of me. I disciplined myself not to turn round and look for my pursuers.

"On race day the hectic blur of competition was my main concern, but as I broke away on 45th Cutting a strange eerie feeling of déjà vu swept over me. "As I had visualized on a number of occasions, so it happened. So powerful and yet spiritual was the sensation that swept over me that I shivered despite Durban's 30°C (86° Fahrenheit) heat, and the hairs on my arms stood up in goose bumps. I had been there before, it was happening just as I had planned it."

When visualizing, pay attention to the following key points:

- **Visualize in the past tense.** Every time you do this exercise, believe that you have already achieved the performance. Why? Research has shown that individuals vary greatly in their ability to actually "see" themselves performing. Some runners are less skilled than others at visualizing. Some cannot do this at all. By visualizing in the past tense, most athletes will have an excellent chance of believing what they are seeing. This is so because they have been conditioned to consider what has happened in the past as relevant to what might happen in the future.

In the weeks prior to his 800-meter personal best, I requested that Ebeneza Felix, an athlete that I coach, spend 10 minutes twice a week, actually telling me how his upcoming race had gone, as if he'd already run it! He'd expressed difficulty visualizing on his own. So I appointed him to be the scriptwriter and director of his own movie. In this movie he was to run the race of his life. He was to explain to me how the story unfolded, in the past tense, for example, "I then swept past everybody in the back straight. I remember feeling surprised at how good I felt at that late stage of the race. The feeling was marvelous. I felt so light and strong!"

- **Focus on actions and process.** Place your emphasis on the desired process, rather than on the outcome. The reason why the emphasis should fall on process is because you have complete control over your attitude while you run, but control over the specific result is not as definite. Much can happen that is beyond your control, and this can alter the outcome, despite your very best efforts.

By focusing on specific actions and the process of running, you are guaranteed to find yourself in familiar territory come race time.

Here are some examples of what you want to experience:
- how your running flows
- how successfully you execute climbs and turns
- how balanced you are
- how good your coordination is
- how easily and effortlessly you run
- how tactically sound you are
- how much of a "natural" you are
- how much you enjoy your participation and success
- how relaxed and rhythmical your breathing is
- how efficiently you run

"Visualizing the race over and over in my mind before it took place, 'seeing' myself pulling away yet still feeling strong, programmed me for a superlative effort. Once the gun went off all I had to do was 'run' the program."

- JOHNNY HALBERSTADT
ONE OF THE ALL TIME GREAT SOUTH AFRICAN RUNNERS, ON HOW HE WON
THE NATIONAL CROSS COUNTRY CHAMPIONSHIPS AGAINST OVERWHELMING ODDS.

- **Form a routine.** For example, tell yourself, "I visualize for 'x' minutes, so many times per week at this specific time."

- **Aim high and be realistic.** Aiming too low will not provide fulfilling results, and setting expectations beyond realistic possibility can be a setup for disappointment. While visualizing, strive to experience a level of running beyond that which you achieve on a regular basis, but avoid "lying" to your sub-conscious. If you've never run a sub 3-hour marathon, don't visualize breaking the world record!

- **Visualize in "real time."** If you are imagining yourself running a mile or a kilometer, put your stop watch on the process and see how close you come to being able to actually visualize at race pace. Initially you will be very inaccurate (too fast!), as you will leave out many details that are actually there when you run. However, as your concentration improves and you fill your imagination with all the details, you will be able to realistically visualize in "real time". This is a very powerful tool.

- **Always "see" success.** The point of visualizing is to imprint your brain with success. Be sure to draw a distinction between visualizing (which must always be successful) and creating mental strategies for possible mishaps and occurrences. Successful visualization is always positive, but there is a definite need to create mental contingency plans.

Sometimes you might visualize a mishap. If this happens, stop the visualization exercise and create an appropriate response to this problem should it really occur. Now redo your visualization exercise from the last start point, ensuring there are no mishaps. "Expect the best, prepare for the worst" is a useful motto in situations like this.

For example, if you see yourself falling at the start of a race, simply imagine yourself getting up and gradually getting back into the race. In this way you have prepared for the mishap and will respond appropriately. It would be good to have an alternative as well, for example, "It's clear I'm too hurt to run, let me get out of here safely, take care of myself and I'll set myself up for another event further down the line."

- **Visualize from your true vantage point: inside yourself.** Be the participant, not a spectator. This means you should be seeing your actual perception while running: the road under your feet, the wind at your back. This is more powerful than observing yourself from a distance.

"I FULLY EXPERIENCE THE RHYTHMICAL FLOW OF MY RUNNING"

VISUALIZATION IN ACTION

Attempt to visualize at least 3 times per week for a total of 12 minutes per session. More is better, but do it a total of at least half an hour per week, even if your sessions are shorter. Just do them more often.

USE THE SECOND PERSON

When you use affirmations in your visualization refer to yourself in the 2nd person. For example, "You run powerfully up the hills. You feel strong toward the finish." This does not indicate that you should see yourself from outside your body, still view your performance as you would as if you were actually running. By addressing yourself in the 2nd person you are more likely to listen to yourself, as the instruction comes across as a command. "Your training is paying off", strongly reminds you of how well you have trained; a positive image.

USE ALL YOUR SENSES

By using ALL your senses (smell, touch, sight, sound and taste) you can design victorious outcomes in your running. By scripting a detailed film in your mind of how you want your runs to occur, you accurately rehearse the actual run.

The only true reality is the one you create. Too often athletes allow circumstances to determine their reality, but by visualizing, you proactively set a scenario to run into, and in doing so, shape your own running destiny.

Examples to imagine:

- The smell of the sports rubs on the runners around you before a race.
- The metallic taste in your mouth when you are running hard.
- The feeling in your stomach produced by supreme effort.
- The sound of clapping and cheering as you near the finish.
- The sight of runners you are passing as you surge toward the top of that final climb.

HAVE CONTINGENCY PLANS

Visualization is so effective that if certain expected conditions don't occur and your plans go awry, unnecessary pressure can be created. To avoid being stuck without an alternative you need to design other solutions. It is also essential to have a flexible mindset so that you can adapt as you go along.

When Joan Benoit-Samuelson set the world record for the marathon in Chicago, she had envisioned perfect racing conditions for the day. This was not to be, and race day dawned grey and dreary. "When I saw that conditions were not conducive to a record, I shelved my plans. But during the race I decided to go for it anyway. So despite pre-determining that conditions would be amazing, and despite not being mentally prepared for the conditions that I did meet, I managed to adapt and set the record."

This is an attribute of so many of the world's great sports people: Even when they have visualized a specific scenario and it doesn't turn out that way, they see themselves as having a positive attitude and possessing a strong sense of commitment to excellence. They believe they are adaptable. With these attributes firmly entrenched in their thinking, they can see themselves succeeding despite awkward circumstances.

VISUALIZATION EXERCISES

I visualize (#) .... per week, at (time) .... am/pm, in (place).....................

You see:

_____

_____

_____

EXAMPLE: *You run smoothly and powerfully with great efficiency*

You taste:

_____

_____

_____

EXAMPLE: *You taste the cool sports drink and experience it fueling your body*

You feel:

_____

_____

_____

EXAMPLE: *You feel capable and light; in control and enjoying the exertion*

You hear:

_____

_____

_____

EXAMPLE: *You hear the footfalls of hundreds of runners as drums spurring you on to triumph*

You smell:

_____

_____

_____

EXAMPLE: *You smell the moisture as it rises off the road at aid stations*

You sense:

_____

_____

_____

EXAMPLE: *You sense your fitness and strength-training paying off*

You experience:

_____

_____

_____

EXAMPLE: *You experience strong feelings of exhilaration and fulfillment as you stride powerfully toward your targets and your destiny*

IMPORTANT

These specific examples are for a race. A run for the purpose of joy, relaxation or some other fulfilling purpose can be created equally effectively through visualizing.

FURTHER USEFUL HINTS & EXAMPLES

Questions to ask:

Have you "seen" how your running career goes?

Have you fully and successfully experienced the next run?

FURTHER EXAMPLES TO HELP YOU VISUALIZE:

Smells and Aromas
- *breakfast before run/race*
- *race drink*
- *rubs/ointments used by runners around you*
- *fresh morning air*

Feelings
- *"butterflies" in stomach*
- *nervous anticipation*
- *tingling at start of your warm-up*
- *cool wind on your face at the start*

Tastes
- *race drinks*
- *dry/cotton mouth before race*
- *breakfast*
- *the metallic taste produced by a hard effort*
- *the drink at the end of a run/race*

Sounds
- *announcements at start*
- *sounds of traffic/vehicles on the way to the start*
- *other competitors*
- *crowds cheering/words of encouragement*
- *blood pumping in your ears*

Visuals

- *the start*
- *loved ones*
- *banners*
- *people*
- *road*
- *competitors*
- *spectators*
- *buildings*
- *finish line*
- *smiling faces*
- *medal*
- *family*

HOW ARE YOU DOING WITH CHAPTER 7?
SEEING YOURSELF RUN AND RACE SUCCESSFULLY

Record the date each time you focus on this component

Date	Date	Date	Date

How do you rate your proficiency with this component?
(Write a date and a score out of five in the block next to the date.)

Rating Scale: 5 = excellent, 4 = good, 3 = acceptable, 2 = poor, 1 = very poor

Date	Score	Date	Score	Date	Score	Date	Score	4 week av.

Comments   (Periodically write down any realizations that you have in this area. How does imagining your runs/races before they actually occur, benefit the quality of each running experience?)

Date

Date

Date

CLEARING

The process of clearing paves the way for the focus required to create and establish all 12 of the components in your running.

By clearing you prioritize and action issues that are confusing you. During these exercises you clear your mind of all that you are currently engaged in. In this way you have a "clean slate" on which to create your running, whether that be to visualize (this chapter), develop a mental strategy (Chapter 9) or any other of the components. This will be done partially when you do the HASE exercise and create operative practices (Chapter 3), but your efforts will be all the more successful if you effectively address the myriad things you have going on in your mind at the time you need to focus fully on something specific.

WHY DO YOU WANT TO BE CLEAR?

Not only are there a great many current issues you have to deal with, there are also past issues that might hold relevance to an upcoming run or race. Just as with current issues, these past issues have to be effectively dealt with, so that you have a clear canvas to paint your upcoming event upon.

It is astounding how having a clear and quiet mind helps you to concentrate. A clear mind is an uncluttered mind. Running while carrying a whole host of concerns allows so little of what you actually have available to be applied. It is like trying to run with a large sack of potatoes over your shoulder, or while holding a precious baby in your arms!

The point of quieting your mind is to set aside the thousand things that otherwise need attention. All these things, large and small, can distract you while you try to focus on developing a new positive habit. Compare it to trying to watch a movie while commercials are being shown all around the screen; it becomes impossible to concentrate!

To achieve this single-mindedness requires that you prioritize all that needs to be done, and put everything down while you handle one thing at a time. Clearing allows you to set down the "commercials" and concentrate on enjoying the movie.

There are two methods that I recommend for effective clearing:

SHARING

Before each challenging run or event, seek out the company of a trusted individual whom you have previously asked to assist you with this process. Each of us has such a person in our lives. It's a good idea to choose someone who is somewhat of a mentor in your life, someone you have a great deal of respect for, and at the same time feel very, very comfortable with. If this is not possible, you can choose a friend for whom you can offer to do the same. Be sure to set the ground rules clearly.

In a private setting, share with that person what is going on in your life. Don't be afraid to really let your feelings show. Vent if you need to: be angry, frustrated or complain, if this makes you feel better. Make sure you mention everything that is on your mind, whether or not it is relevant to the upcoming event. This is the time to judge, to complain and to whine if you want!

The only thing the friend, family member or mentor has to do is listen. They should never allow themselves to get sucked in by what you are saying. At best they can objectively repeat what you are saying, with the sole purpose of reassuring you that they have heard and understood you. For example, your comment of "I really don't have the mileage to do this marathon," might be answered with, "I understand that you believe you've not trained enough for this race."

Doing this exercise is not necessarily for you to hear answers or receive solutions. Often there are not any immediate solutions. You would not really be voicing certain concerns if you were actively sorting them out. The purpose is to get things off your chest and to hear yourself. We all need to be heard, and once this is done we usually feel better.

When you truly hear yourself, your problems tend to become finite and manageable. This happens because by voicing what's on your mind you shift the perspective from an internal "in your head" point of view, to something out in front of you. A number of the issues and concerns you raise might not be problems at all, just items that are part of what's on your plate and that need attention.

Having the issue on the table in plain view and having another person there alters the perspective significantly. It becomes easier to be objective with yourself and see solutions that you would offer others were they to ask you to help them. You also see how pointless and/or damaging some of your interpretations are. Notice how some of your judgments hurt you. See opportunities to replace these poor interpretations with ones that inspire and motivate you.

As with training, the more regularly you do this, the better you become. As your skill increases, you will open up more and more. As this happens the process becomes increasingly valuable. Learn to enjoy the feeling of getting all that "stuff" off your chest. Also appreciate how much clearer your thinking is once you've done this.

LISTING

This second method is another process through which your mind can set aside distractions. It works well either on your own or in a group setting under the guidance of a coach or assistant. Unlike sharing, which works excellently just before a race, this method works best before a target (Chapter 4) and goal-setting (Chapter 5) exercise, and especially before a visualization exercise (this chapter). Listing should be done as often as possible. By developing a routine this exercise becomes ingrained and eventually forms a habit.

How to do listing:

- Sit at a desk or table in a quiet, darkened room.

- Bend your knees and place your feet apart and relaxed.

- Place your hands about shoulder width apart, palms down, on the table.

- Take a few slow, deep breaths. Imagine your mind quieting and your body relaxing and being cleansed as you breathe out.

- Close your eyes and relax the muscles of your face.

- Imagine you are sitting at a window looking into the farthest distance you can see. You notice only shapes and colors. Perhaps you see mountains of purple and a sky of blue, perhaps the dark blue of the ocean and lighter blue of the sky.

- Then bring your focus slightly closer. Imagine more distinct shapes. Perhaps notice individual peaks, or perhaps a peninsula or island or ships away in the distance.

- Then bring your focus even closer. Perhaps you can see individual houses, buildings, trees, cars, colors and larger advertising billboards. You can see vehicles moving and perhaps even people, but no clear detail.

- Now bring your focus to the foreground. You see the street in front of you, or something equally close, you see different kinds of trees, maybe a cat or dog, a wheelbarrow or a garden hose and individual shrubs.

- Finally focus on the interior and immediate vicinity of the room where you are sitting. See the color and type of curtains, the texture and substance of the surface your hands are on. Notice other details on the desk: books, calendars etc. Notice a writing pad and pen or pencil. Is the paper lined? What are the dimensions of the pad? Is it a pen or pencil? What color is it? If it is a pen what color is the ink?

- In your imagination pick up the pen or pencil and begin to quickly write on the paper all that is currently occupying your mind—anything: relationships, work, friends, bills to pay, the race coming up, financial issues and concerns, birthdays, vehicle maintenance, etc.

- Once you are sure you have written all that is on your mind or in your thoughts, good or bad, fold the sheet(s) of paper. Notice how you fold it (them), how many times and into what shape.

- Now "turn around" and "see" (with your mind's eye) a box or container of some sort, close at hand. You are going to place the list in this container that you have specifically chosen for this purpose. Give the holder color, texture and dimensions. What is it made of? Does it have a slit in the lid, is it hinged, or is it a loose lid?

- Place your list in this special container.

- As you do so promise yourself that you will attend to whatever remains relevant on that list at a fixed time after your race or run.

You should now have a clear mind and be in a super-relaxed state, ready to visualize or create any part of your upcoming event. You MUST return to your list as you promised yourself. By not honoring this agreement, you undermine the trust you have for yourself.

Clearing is about gaining and regaining control of your thinking. In this way your mind has space and calmness, allowing you to think clearly and narrow your focus sufficiently so as to exercise the full power of your influence and to get what you want.

REPROGRAMMING YOUR SUB-CONSCIOUS MIND

Your rational mind does not simply store information as you perceive it with your senses. Everything that you experience gets interpreted by your conscious mind—you first judge it, and then act upon that interpretation.

For example, should you live on the west coast of the United States and travel to the east coast for a race, the following might happen: Someone tells you that the time change is going to affect your race negatively. You will either decide (interpret) that it will affect you, or you'll decide that you are not affected by time changes and you'll be just fine. Although there are some real physiological considerations that need to be addressed, by far the greatest effect will be generated by what you believe. This belief is a judgment, not a fact.

Your sub-conscious mind works on a different premise. It does not interpret: it simply stores facts as perceived. If, for example, you were to berate yourself for forgetting to bring your running shoes to a race by calling yourself a stupid fool, your sub-conscious would simply record that you called yourself a stupid fool. Like a tape recorder, the next time you made an error, the words "stupid fool" would be readily available. The more it happened, the more the epithet would stick. Eventually you forget that it's simply something you once said and become the "stupid fool" you keep calling yourself.

REPLACING BEHAVIORS

Consider your sub-conscious mind as a sponge. It will absorb anything you put into it and give it right back when you are under pressure. The only way to erase what you have programmed into the sub-conscious is to replace the information. Now that you are conscious of the choice, ensure that this new information is what you want to store.

For example, the words, "As a marathoner, I'm not fast enough to be competitive in 10K races", get replaced by constantly affirming yourself with the words: "With my endurance as a marathoner and my increased strength work, I am a force to be reckoned with over the shorter distances."

This is why affirmations are so powerful. It is also why affirmations do not need to be believed for them to be so effective. The sub-conscious mind does not judge. This also explains why the idea of trying to change what is currently a poor interpretation in your estimation is often futile. In other words it is far easier to completely delete an old ineffective way of thinking by consciously adopting a different, effective mindset.

By attempting to change the weak belief, you are actually focusing on it and therefore reinforcing it. The interpretation lies in your conscious mind, the "fact" of how you see yourself, lies in the sub-conscious. This fact can therefore only be replaced in the sub-conscious mind by inserting another fact and in this way deleting the old way, (see Chapter 1).

As stated previously, the sub-conscious mind can be likened to a sponge or a tape recorder. It records information accurately, but unlike the conscious mind that interprets what it receives, the sub-conscious mind does not judge or comment on what it records. When required to, the sub-conscious gives back exactly what it recorded. When you call yourself a "silly idiot" for going out to fast in a race, your conscious mind knows that this is only in a manner of speaking. Your sub-conscious mind however recorded that you are an idiot! When you are under pressure you recall this damaging memory. Do this enough times and it affects the way you perceive yourself as a runner. Sadly it seems to be the style of many western cultures to demean themselves. I hear it with runners all the time, "I'm useless, I'm fat, I'll never get fit in time, I'm too slow, I'm too old, I can't run hills." The list is endless. Start becoming aware of how you pre-program your mind, and use this awareness to put powerful self-supporting beliefs into your sub-conscious. You'll thank me next time the going gets tough.

The only way in which you can delete these harmful bits of information is to record over them, by replacing the contents of the sub-conscious sponge with new appropriate messages. The concept of replacing certain behaviors instead of attempting to alter or repair old ones works very effectively.

DEFUSING THE POWER OF THE PAST

Accept that no past running event has any direct bearing on any future run. What happened is over, and has no control over what's to come. Things that pop into your mind, like fear or feelings of inadequacy before a race, do not exist in the reality of the moment. They are creations constructed in the past, and only you allow them to influence your current thinking and choices. The first and greatest step in this process is to distinguish when and how this happens. As soon as you notice this, half the battle is won!

For example, if you see a rival warming up whom you did not expect in the race, you might begin to feel the same feelings of doubt you encountered last time and remember the result, which to your recollection and interpretation was exceedingly poor. By focusing on what can go wrong, you very effectively bring about the mental and physiological changes that will effect the result you fear. In effect, you've set a self-fulfilling, negative prophecy in motion.

If you try to block this negative thinking it will grow worse! (Ever try to fall asleep when you couldn't? The harder you tried the more wide-awake you became!) Our minds are like computers: They cannot comprehend the concept "not." Should you ask a computer not to search for something it will do exactly the opposite, and find those things it recognizes in your request. This is because there is no real command to do something. One cannot "not" do something. If you ask a child to not do something, you create a quandary for that child; what must he or she then do? That's why it's more helpful to frame thoughts in positive constructions. For example, saying to yourself that you should conserve your energy in the opening stages of a race, has far more influence on your actions than saying you must not go out too fast. All that this negative statement does is access a program in your mind on how to go out too fast!

Understanding this provides insight into why, on occasion, despite your most concerted and passionate efforts, things don't work out the way you had planned. When you focus on what you don't want, you get what you don't want. Remember, "What you resist will persist."

REMOVE ALL RESISTANCE

To further illustrate the example of the archrival arriving unexpectedly, when you say: "Don't worry about so-and-so, he/she won't affect my race," you will be concerned about so-and-so and it will affect your race. Because that is in essence what you are focusing on and asking yourself to do!

Instead, try this: "I see so-and-so's here. I acknowledge the thoughts I have about that. I am aware of my interpretations and judgments around this fact. I choose to focus on how I run my own race."

In this way you remove the resistances and fears you have of things happening that you don't want and focus on what you do want. When you let go of your resistances, they will disappear.

So next time you encounter one of your old foes out on the road, be it the hills themselves or an opponent, let go of the need to confront and withstand, to battle and resist. Focus rather on feeling strong or being assertive. In this way you regain power and control and are able to effect real influence on what you do desire. The steps to take are as follows:

- Allow the negative thoughts that arise in your mind. Observe them for what they are. They are only thoughts. If you do this they will pass, because you have not judged them to be the truth about you. If you attempt to shut out or block these thoughts for fear of them damaging your performance, they will become your truth about the matter and have a significant and powerfully negative impact on your running.

• Focus on the task at hand and what you want.

• Get in touch with how well you trained and the knowledge of how ready you are for this (if this is the case). If not, focus on how you've always got through such situations. If it is a first time, recall other instances where your positive mindset pulled you through.

• Logically confirm your true ability.

• Strictly execute your pre-planned warm-up routine in minute detail. Ensure that you repeat your affirmations (Chapter 2); clearly seed feelings of success (Chapter 8); visualize important segments of the run (this chapter); run through your targets (Chapter 4); and clearly become your goals (Chapter 5). We do all this anyway; we need only structure it positively.

• Refer to your race mission (Chapter 6); see that this race has value to you and others (Chapter 12); know that you have practiced and have the skills to deal with all and any challenges (Chapter 11) and choose to enjoy and learn from this event as part of your lifetime commitment to running (Chapter 10). Feel assured by the knowledge that by staying in each moment (yes, even the moment of your perceived fear), you grow and live fully. This is why you run—to be challenged and take on these challenges with joyful vigor (Chapter 13).

"MY MIND IS CLEAR AND UNCLUTTERED"
"I AM FREE TO RUN"

RELAXATION

TENSION

Mental stress causes physical contraction in voluntary muscle fiber. This tension tightens antagonistic muscles, the muscles that are not doing the work, and causes the prime movers, the muscles that are doing the work, to strain against this inhibiting force. This blockage brings about premature fatigue. It's like trying to straighten your leg while someone else holds it bent. You grow tired very quickly. Runners who suffer from tension are often surprised at how quickly they grow tired in races, as they can continue far more comfortably in training at the same pace.

Another unfortunate side effect of tension that haunts many runners is diarrhea. This performance-robbing stomach condition can be prevented by learning to quiet your fear, as has been explained, and relaxing.

As my Tai C'hi teacher always says, there is a difference between *relaxing* and *collapsing*. When you relax you maintain good posture, when you collapse, you slouch and shuffle, actually creating more tension.

STRETCHING

Due to the nature of running, your muscles, especially in the legs, tend to become very strong and as a result they shorten. To counteract this requires regular stretching, especially after exercise. Stretching helps to ensure that you recover quickly, remain injury free and keep your muscles supple for the activity you love.

To be able to stretch effectively, you must be able to relax. And to relax your muscles requires that you calm your mind. Tension shows up in your body as taught muscles. It therefore makes sense to first become mentally relaxed before physical activity. You will achieve a degree of muscle release through clearing alone. You can then improve relaxation and flexibility further, by stretching. Be sure however, to run or walk for a few minutes before commencing with your stretching routine. You need to increase blood flow to the muscles and increase their core temperature to make them more elastic.

The ability to relax is crucial for success in athletics. Relaxation is important not only in racing, but in training, stretching, resting, mental preparation and more.

The point to strive for in your stretching is to have it become an enjoyable process of self-nurturing, peace and total relaxation; something that you do for it's own sake, not "in order to."

The two processes described for "clearing" earlier in the chapter both serve as extremely effective mental relaxation drills and are wonderful precursors to the processes of progressively relaxing your muscles. It is therefore advisable to use one of those activities before you proceed with the muscle relaxation drills.

FACILITATION

Like massage, total body relaxation can "de-facilitate" the muscles and leave you feeling relaxed, but sluggish. This is why sharing is good before an event, but listing better before visualization and affirmation sessions. Before an event you need to be in a state of peak awareness and appropriate facilitation, being relaxed and ready, "keyed-up", but not tense. Having this knowledge and awareness will soon teach you the appropriate, optimal level of readiness to ensure a peak performance. Use each successful endeavor as an addition to your "memory bank" of how it feels to be in that optimum zone. This makes it easier to achieve that ideal performance state on subsequent efforts. (See Chapter 8).

The nature of racing is such that most runners are too tense before an event anyway and can afford to be as relaxed as they possibly can.

UNDERSTAND ANXIETY – ALLOW PERFORMANCE

It is important to fully grasp the mechanics of how pre-event nervousness affects performance. Part of human design is to have us be instantly ready for massive physical activity. This no doubt stems from our origins as pre-historic man when situations of extreme bodily danger arose in an instant. For example, our ancestors might have been peacefully ambling down a narrow canyon when suddenly confronted by a saber-toothed tiger. They needed to instantly be capable of either escape or self-defense. Because of that, humans have been equipped with a set of glands, called the adrenal glands, which elicit what is called a "fight or flight response". This is a complex series of bio-chemical actions that instantly prepare you for action:

- Pupils dilate to see more clearly.
- Blood vessels to working muscles open up to allow oxygen-rich blood.
- The heart beats faster and more forcefully to provide that blood.
- Breathing dramatically increases to oxygenate the increased blood supply for the release of energy.
- Senses become hyper-aware to perceive all the information needed for protection.
- Blood sugar levels rise to fuel this heightened demand for the energy sapping activity that lies immediately ahead.
- Blood pressure increases as part of this readiness to act.

Now all this is good and well if it happens when you need it. (Think: "Who expected a woolly mammoth with those threatening tusks on that frozen ledge this morning?!") But that reaction becomes a problem when you know about the beasties you must face, weeks and even months in advance. In fact, in modern society, chances are you know exactly when you are going to encounter danger or excitement.

For example, you know that that 10K race is a month from now on that specific date, at that precise hour, in front of all those people, against so-and-so who always beats you. The disadvantage of knowing this is that all these defense or attack processes can be set in motion every time you even think of your upcoming race. When this happens, and there is no physical activity to use all the accompanying facilitatory processes, the body and mind are in a great quandary. There is no physical action to be taken right then. In other words, the body is ready for fight or flight, only to find neither—causing an undesirable overload. The body then shuts down the unnecessary heightened readiness.

This is extremely taxing on the system—rather like preparing for a race and then arriving at the start line only to hear that the event has been cancelled. Such an anti-climax will leave you all hyped with no physical activity to serve as a catharsis. You can't unload, and you suffer the consequences. Over a period of time this can wear you down and has been shown to exacerbate stress related conditions such as ulcers, migraines, high blood pressure, asthma and other nervous disorders.

THE INSULIN REACTION

It is believed that to a runner, probably the most detrimental short-term effect of a fight or flight response without physical activity, is that your blood sugar levels become too elevated. To counteract this excess of blood sugar, your pancreas secretes insulin, which breaks down the excess glucose. The downside of this, however, is that even though you won't now go into a coma and even possibly die (as diabetics without insulin can do), your energy is sapped for a while. You feel lame, weak and woozy. I'm sure you might have experienced that all too familiar feeling before an important event and said something like, "Oh no! I feel horrible, where did my energy go? I really don't feel capable of racing right now!"

There are two ways to effectively combat this performance robbing reaction:

REINTERPRETATION

Prevention is better than cure. By having a clear understanding of the fight or flight syndrome and knowing how and when it happens and recognizing its onset, you can defuse the situation by using affirmations (Chapter 2) that counter such a reaction, like:

- "I am calm and relaxed"
- "I am excited and in control"
- "I love to race"
- "I look forward to the thrill of racing"
- "This is what I've trained for"
- "I am mentally and physically calm and ready"
- "I enjoy the rush of excitement"

Rationalize the source of your apprehension and fear by re-interpreting the value and meaning of the race. In this way you re-frame what you are dealing with and it becomes infinitely easier to imagine. For example, by knowing and telling yourself it's only a half-marathon that you've run many times before; it's a race you know well and enjoy; you've trained well and you are ready, you give the experience finite, measurable, understandable parameters.

Once you assure yourself that you can get your head around something, the vague fear that comes from irrational interpretation dissipates. Once the monster under the bed of a 6-year-old becomes only a dressing gown in a heap, the angst is gone. Create relief for yourself by talking and thinking clearly, rationally and objectively about an upcoming event.

PHYSICAL ACTION

If it's too late and you realize you are so rigged from nerves you can hardly move, do the following: Get physically active, and do so fast!

Seriously, all that adrenalin and blood sugar with no action is bad for you—the very cause of the problem—so GO! GO! GO! Get striding, run it off, do an active mobility/stretching and facilitation routine. (An effective warm-up routine involves not only stretching exercises, but running and various other physical activities that require concentration and energy.) Both concentration on and execution of complex physical activities utilize blood sugar as an energy source and assist in maintaining optimum blood sugar levels.

Really focus on your pre-race routine in detail. Stay in the moment and follow the procedure as laid out in reinterpretation above. This will sufficiently burn off excess blood sugar so as to prevent the dreaded insulin response.

In events of marathon length and longer, ensure that you do not get too nervous, as too much activity can burn precious glycogen that you will need on the road when the going gets long. To avoid nervousness before long races, focus on the many little details that require attention: your socks, shoes, stretches, pace and so on. This can keep you from projecting to the "saber-tooth" part of the race that is still in the future.

HOW TO RELAX

I have recommended three exercises. These have been laid out in the ensuing pages. They can be practiced in conjunction with each other. It is recommended that you do a clearing exercise (see earlier in this chapter) first, as it is easier to focus when your mind is calm. This results in a much deeper level of physical relaxation. It is suggested that you do these exercises in the sequence in which they appear. Each one will bring about a progressively more relaxed state.

It is also possible to do these exercises individually, as there are times when you need a quick breathing space to gather your thoughts, relax and be ready to run.

Being nervous or tense is often associated with hyperventilation. This is when you forget to breathe out. This condition can quickly be alleviated if you are conscious of the fact that you are doing it. All you need to do is breathe out or exhale fully and then allow your breathing to get back to a rhythmical, controlled pattern.

However, you might find yourself in such a state of panic that you need outside assistance. Often breathing into a paper bag helps. As the amount of oxygen in the bag decreases, you should be able to get the breathing pattern back to normal—the increase in carbon dioxide triggers the process.

Breathe out consciously once in a while when running hard. This helps restore your breathing rhythm and relaxes you.

BREATH AWARENESS

The first relaxation drill also involves breath consciousness. Most successful relaxation procedures use breathing as a basis for the exercise.

- Become aware of your breathing. Realize that you can have it be slow or rapid, deep or shallow, into your stomach or into your chest. You can even stop it all together. You have complete control over it. Enjoy and appreciate this mastery.

- If you are practiced you can even become aware of your heartbeat and also slow it down. This too is an excellent method to become focused, relaxed and calm.

- Imagine your inhalation providing your lungs with energy-giving oxygen. Envisage your heart pumping this oxygen-rich blood to your furthest extremities. Also, see these long controlled breaths reaching throughout your body and calming you.

- Imagine crisp, fresh, clear, clean air coming into your body, and then slowly exhale air that is gray, cloudy and dull, carrying with it all the impurities and waste-products of your aerobic metabolism. Imagine breathing to be a cleansing and supporting activity.

- Focus intently upon your breathing and its wonderful value. This will narrow your focus and remove unwanted thoughts and concerns that cause your muscles to tense and your body to become rigid and inflexible. Do this until you feel the benefits.

- A few deep, controlled breaths before a run or race bring you right back to where you should be for a great experience—calm, focused, relaxed and in control.

- It often helps if you close your eyes while doing this, as the eyes take in all the frenetic activity around you, and this makes it difficult to relax.

- Similarly, by blocking out discordant and disturbing sounds through either retiring to a quiet place, putting on headphones with soothing sounds or music, or simply closing your ears, you create an environment where breath-awareness and control is easier.

- As with all activities of this nature, success requires practice and adaptation to suit each individual. As you master the skill, you will gain more and more benefit.

CONTRACT AND RELAX

The second exercise also requires a quiet, safe and comfortable setting. Again, as you gain experience and confidence you find that you can do these drills even when chaos reigns around you.

- The first principle of relaxation is awareness. You cannot relax a specific part of your body, unless you are aware of how it feels when it is tense. Tense the area you wish to relax and then let it go. In this way you actually experience the physical sensation of relaxing.

  If for example, you are running along and someone shouts, "relax your shoulders", shrug them up real tightly and then let them go and allow them to become loose or relaxed. After all you would not consciously run with tense shoulders, would you?

- Do this kind of "body check" regularly, especially with hands, arms, shoulders, neck and face and lower back (to prevent arching). A good way to relax is to sit or lie quietly and attempt to contract and relax each body area that has voluntary muscle, one at a time. Move from the furthest extremities towards the center (your chest and stomach). Begin with each foot individually (or even your toes); then hands; calves and shins; forearms; thighs; upper arms; glutes (butt muscles) and pelvis; face and neck; shoulders and back; chest and stomach. Remember practice makes perfect. You will discover new and pleasant sensations and a level of relaxation you would hardly have believed possible.

- This exercise also increases your perceptual-motor awareness. You discover how out of touch you are (or how in touch you are!) with individual muscle groups and how good or poor your ability is to relax/communicate with these areas. Such body awareness greatly enhances your running efficiency. Mastering this exercise ensures that you do not unnecessarily contract or hold tense muscles that do not support your running or posture. When you learn this skill your running gait is freed up to flow smoothly and powerfully. Learning how to specifically relax while running will efficiently support your unique running style.

VISUALIZED MUSCLE RELAXATION

The third and final drill is more specific and requires a certain level of mastery and understanding of the first two. In this exercise you use your imagination to progressively relax your muscles.

- Imagine you are lying in the warm (safe!) sun on the beach and your muscles are made of butter. Experience first the muscles of each foot softening, growing slowly heavy and fluid and then melting off your foot and seeping into the sand. Then do your hands and fingers; then your shins and calves; then your forearms and wrists; then your knees; your shoulders; then your thighs (hamstrings and quads); face and neck; glutes (butt) and pelvis muscles; upper back; hips; lower back and then finally stomach and chest.

- In this way, with good imagination, you should be able to effectively relax and ready yourself for efficient running.

- In the same vein you can use the image of lying in a bath and having warm cement poured over you. Imagine the concrete solidifying around you. Again, work from the extremities inward. (Some runners feel a little claustrophobic with this exercise. They visualize so well that they become afraid of being stuck and smothered in the cement! For this reason you can also use warm mud or clay as an image.)

- Relaxed muscles are more flexible, able to contract more powerfully, are not as easily injured, are more efficient, recover far more rapidly and feel just plain good.

"I KNOW HOW TO RELAX AND DO SO"

THE RUNNING GROOVE
ACCESSING YOUR PERFORMANCE ZONE

*"We all have the power. Our thoughts create
our reality, and seeding is merely working with the
thought that you already have the thing that you want."*
- JOHN KEHOE

ALLOW YOUR ACTIONS TO DETERMINE HOW YOU FEEL

Although it seemingly defies logic, most people act according to how they feel, and not according to the facts of a situation. That means people tend to automatically respond to occurrences based on their emotions at the time. This pattern can be turned around to great effect by deciding instead that your actions can determine how you feel. That means you can commit to an excellent level of running, no matter how you feel.

Have you ever noticed when you go to a party that no matter how you feel, pretty soon everybody else's good mood starts to affect you positively? People often rely on such external events to put them in a happy state. In extreme cases, such an inability to create one's own feelings of well being can even lead to drug and alcohol abuse, and other destructive, compulsive, addictive behaviors.

Other people, however, take greater responsibility for their frame of mind. Great runners, for example, can and do create a zone for themselves in which they feel capable of performing at the highest level. In this "ideal performance state," they let go and allow the magic to happen. They set the right frame of mind, and then allow the running to flow from them.

Sally Edwards, a pioneer in the sport of triathlon and author of several books on athletic training, clearly recalls the day she discovered how it felt to enter that magical state of performance beyond the physical.

"My goal for Ironman in 1990 was to achieve master's records in four Ironman races on different continents. In the final of the four races, in Hawaii, after the bike leg (at the start of the marathon), I was 21 minutes behind my nemesis, and her strength was her running!

"There came a moment during the marathon when I had reached the point of absolute exhaustion—the high heat and winds had taken their toll (when physically it seemed over). I knew that I had to shake the weariness. Then slowly, I felt a strange, difficult-to-explain rush of sensation—I call it the "sweet spot" in sport. It was as if everything were coming together and the exhaustion were being let go; it was a feeling of possibility, blended with a sense of hope. I started to feel better, I picked up the pace, and I was joyfully conscious that what was happening was a rare phenomenon."

Edwards finished the race having made up 12 of those 21 minutes and went home treasuring that precious moment when, as she put it, "the master's woman ahead of me ended up beating me by 9 minutes in 11 hours of racing. Yet I took that moment—the 'sweet spot'—as mine. Both the victory and the defeat were what I made of them, and I left the experience with hope (for further such magic) for the future."

FIND YOUR "SWEET SPOT" AT WILL

Cease from believing that those periods of excellent, blissful running are just lucky breaks or flukes. Such times indicate your TRUE ABILITY. To run in the ideal mental state is possible far more often than the average runner reports. This state of mind, the one that produces great athletic achievements, is often referred to as the Zone.

I have a very gregarious friend, Dr. Sibis Mouton, who is a prime example of an athlete who achieves an ideal performance state every time she competes. She is an international and age-group winner of both the world ultra distance triathlon championships (Nice, 1998), and the world ultra duathlon champs (Zofingen, 1999). Before and after races she is a jovial and extroverted individual who has a kind and laughing word for all she sees. During an event she becomes an automaton who sees and hears nothing around her. She remains narrowly focused on the task at hand and always produces a performance equal to or surpassing the form she displays in training. Her immense concentration is further shown by her ability to give a detailed account of how the entire event unfolded for her. This ability to alter her mindset at will explains how she has remained competitive throughout a career that has spanned 25 years.

To place yourself in this powerful performance Zone where dream running comes true you need to recall in graphic detail your best performances and most enjoyable, exciting times. These need not necessarily be only running experiences, but can include occasions such as your graduation, your first car, your first child, or when you received a prize, reward or accolade or reached some other meaningful milestone.

REMEMBER HOW YOU FELT. EXPERIENCE FULLY AGAIN THAT SAME FEELING BEFORE THE RUN THAT LIES AHEAD.

*"This 'bubble' state only comes two or three times
in a marathoner's career, and this baffles me, for I am sure
an athlete can acquire this bubble state more times than three."*

- PRISCILLA WELCH, ON BEING IN THE ZONE

When you recall such occasions, the body releases "feel-good" hormones like endorphins, which pre-set your physiology and mind for a euphoric, fulfilling running experience. It is an exercise that puts both the body and mind in an optimal state of excitement and heightened preparedness.

Research has indicated that when runners imagine or are shown videos of themselves involved in enjoyable or successful experiences, their body chemistry and muscles react. This response helps create an effective mood for what is to come. It's like watching an exciting or emotional film, you begin to become involved physically and mentally. Reading or thinking of a proposed race scenario for an upcoming event can achieve the same effect. This physiological response powerfully facilitates you and ensures a state of mental and physical readiness that can lead to an exceptional running experience.

"I FEEL GOOD BECAUSE I SAY SO"

"I AM ALWAYS READY TO RUN MY BEST BECAUSE I CLEARLY RECALL AND USE MY PREVIOUS SUCCESSES"

CREATING YOUR OWN RUNNING GROOVE

IT IS RECOMMENDED THAT YOU BE CLEAR AND RELAXED BEFORE BEGINNING THESE EXERCISES. (See Clearing, Relaxation and How to Relax in Chapter 7.)

Before each run ensure that you are in an optimal state. Do this by remembering the occasions in your life when everything was perfect and everything fell into place in a balanced and successful way. You experienced joy and fulfillment. These experiences are:

1. _____

_____

_____

_____

EXAMPLES: *Crossing the finish line of my first race*
The birth of my child

2. _____

_____

_____

_____

EXAMPLES: *When I walked down the aisle and received my diploma*
When I met my life partner

3. _____

_____

_____

_____

EXAMPLE: *I helped someone overcome something successfully*

4. _____

_____

_____

_____

EXAMPLE: *My first overseas trip*

Now, using your examples, record in as much detail as possible how each felt. Recall the emotions and feelings of joy, happiness, satisfaction, fulfillment, bliss, love, success etc.. Please note, the examples given in this excercise coincide with the examples in the previous excercise.

1. _____

_____

_____

_____

EXAMPLES: *I felt so proud and relieved*
　　　　　　　I was overwhelmed by the miracle of life

2. _____

_____

_____

_____

EXAMPLES: *I felt proud and excited about the future*
My heart kept beating madly

3. _____

_____

_____

_____

EXAMPLE: *I experienced a deep sense of appreciation and fulfillment*

4. _____

_____

_____

_____

EXAMPLE: *I was extremely excited, filled with anticipation and a little scared!*

FURTHER USEFUL HINTS & EXAMPLES

Questions to ask:

Can you get into an effective running mindset whenever you need to?

Can you get into the Zone in every important race?

FURTHER EXAMPLES OF POSSIBLE RECOLLECTIONS THAT PUT YOU IN THE ZONE:

- *A great past race*
- *A moment of excellence in another sport*
- *A completed fulfilling project*
- *An exciting adventure*
- *A new home*
- *A highly successful business deal*
- *Winning a competition*
- *A roller-coaster ride*

HOW ARE YOU DOING WITH CHAPTER 8?
ACCESSING YOUR PERFORMANCE ZONE

Record the date each time you focus on this component

Date	Date	Date	Date

How do you rate your proficiency with this component?
(Write a date and a score out of five in the block next to the date.)

Rating Scale: 5 = excellent, 4 = good, 3 = acceptable, 2 = poor, 1 = very poor

Date	Score	Date	Score	Date	Score	Date	Score	4 week av.

Comments   (Periodically write down any realizations you have in this area. How does re-experiencing other enjoyable, successful endeavors place you in a mood that ensures that you are in an exceptional frame of mind for your upcoming running experience?)

Date

Date

Date

STRATEGIC RUNNING
PLANNING THE PERFECT RUNNING EXPERIENCE

*"Life doesn't necessarily work according to plan,
but it doesn't work at all without a plan."*
– AGON ZARD

IMPORTANT

Read and execute this section in conjunction with Chapter 2. That way you will know how to create and word the affirmations that form an integral part of your running strategy.

To understand how to get psychologically strong is one thing, but to actually design and put into practice such a plan is something completely different. Success can only occur through action.

KNOWLEDGE VS. KNOWING

There is a great difference between *knowledge* and *knowing*. Knowledge is a recollection of something you studied or heard. Knowing adds the element of understanding to that equation. In running it is required that you deeply know and believe that you have the ability. Your knowing must be there when you need it, because you have practiced it a thousand times. You believe that the skill, the fitness and you, the runner, are one. You and your running have become indistinguishable. When people say, "Look at that runner's unbelievable instinct, everything just happens so fluidly, as if he/she isn't even trying very hard," you know that such a level of running has been achieved.

CONTROLLING YOUR INTERNAL DIALOGUE

We all have a little voice that chatters incessantly in our heads. It's the voice that tells you that you are tired, or slow, or not fit, or running badly. It has something to say about everything you experience. Somehow this internal voice does not seem to have your best interests at heart! Its greatest desire is to judge and have its predictions validated. "You can't run that fast!" it says, and then after a poor performance, "I told you so."

When you are relaxed and in control you can work around these interjections. But when you are at your most vulnerable, tired or disheartened, these thoughts can be devastating.

This need not be so! Instead, you can pre-plan your self-talk so that you tell the voice what you want to hear. In this way, when you find yourself under pressure, you will receive the messages you need. The voice will always be there, so you might as well use it to best effect. Accept that it will either hurt your running, or aid it. Choose the latter.

POSITIVE SELF-TALK

Many of the world's top runners have turned their careers around by altering the content of their internal dialogue. In 1996 Colleen De Reuck was selected to represent her country in the world cross-country championships. At that time there was only one women's race, the 6K. (Now there are two, a 4K and an 8K). In this championship, the best women in the world from track, cross-country and road racing meet in one race to determine who is best. At that time Colleen's best position had been in the high 20's, yet her road racing performances indicated that she should perform better.

A week before the championship race I discovered that she considered herself just "one of the girls," (her own words), but definitely not one of the best. In the course of the next five days we worked on her considering herself as a likely winner of the event. All went well until the morning of the race. In a conversation that we had while she was warming up to do some pre-race striding, she said to me, "I hope I beat Zola (Budd-Pieterse, the South African who had won the world cross-country champs twice as a British citizen)." Zola, who is a good friend of Colleen's, was just coming off the birth of her first child and not remotely in as good a shape as Colleen at the time. Zola would not be a contender for the title. Could I turn around Colleen's relapse to a mediocre mindset in such a brief space of time? Thankfully, before the race Colleen did acknowledge that the time had come to consider herself as world class and that the only way she had any hope of winning a medal was to run to win.

She did just that, taking the lead at the midpoint of the race and ending up in 5th place with the same time as the bronze medallist. In the post-race press conference she told the ecstatic South African press that she had finally listened to her coach and decided that if everyone else considered her to be world class, she had to believe it herself.

The result confirmed that the self-talk first had to alter, then the results would follow.

CREATE YOUR OWN KEYS

Accomplished running not only requires good training, confidence and visualization, but also planning. The mental planning strategy employed in this program is to connect each physical situation with a key phrase that brings about the appropriate frame of mind for that specific situation. These keys are predetermined, learned words and phrases intended to instantaneously place you in a highly effective mental state for your running. Then, when a specific situation arises, you will be able to recognize it, determine what is required and say your key phrases. This leads to the correct behavior. For example, the thought, "I am 20 seconds off the pace" is answered with: "I perform best under pressure." This immensely increases your confidence. Practice this until it becomes automatic.

The fact is that you already do this kind of thinking, but unfortunately mostly in the negative. "I am behind," is usually followed with, "Oh shucks, now I'd better do something or I'm going to lose/be disappointed/not run my target time." This leads to a loss of confidence and focus that leads to ineffective running.

Just as each moment and run is predetermined and trained for, so too there should be "keys" for each situation. These keys should ensure the best psychological mindset and bring about effective, joyful running. Plan the content of your thoughts, for they give birth to your actions.

To determine the mental and physical paths of successful running requires that we map the way we intend to go by laying out each step. This means creating and executing the actions and then adding the words, thoughts and phrases that ensure successful mindsets along the way.

For example, "When I reach the hills I become a mountain goat, effortlessly bounding to the top. I have trained and am ready for this. I'm excited about trying out my new-found mental powers."

Break down each run, each race and your running in general this way, creating a physical and mental map of the steps of successful running.

MOVING FROM SUBJECTIVE TO OBJECTIVE THOUGHTS

Running is an automatic activity, which operates under the principle of the *extensor-cross reflex*. This means that movement is not initiated in the brain, but is a reflex action in the spine. When it comes to pre-planning your thought content, this is very significant. Should your thoughts initially be of an objective or technical nature, they would interfere with your automatic, reflexive flow. For example, the brain would attempt to insert them into your natural flowing movement, causing it to become jerky and unnatural. By attempting to swing your arms just right, or by trying to keep your stride low to the ground, you would use unnecessary energy and disrupt your natural gait. The less you interfere with your automatic running style, the more flowing and efficient your running will be.

When you are fresh, your pre-planned thought strategy and self-talk should be subjective in nature and you should say things to yourself that address your feelings, mood, or flow. For example, think "I am loose and light. I feel fit, strong and relaxed. I am floating along like a seagull. I am controlled and fast. I am a gazelle." Allow your natural flowing style, formed by countless runs, to dictate your form. Don't try, just be.

Only when fatigue causes your form to deteriorate should you insert objective, mechanical thoughts such as: "Use your arms, push away forcibly with your feet, relax your face, drop your chin." It is when you stop running in a fresh and relaxed manner that you need your brain to tell your body to run correctly, not before.

See "FURTHER USEFUL HINTS & EXAMPLES" at the end of this chapter for more ideas and a detailed example of a pre-race mental strategy.

"I HANDLE ANY SITUATION BY CHOOSING MY THOUGHTS"

PLANNING THE PERFECT RUN

IT IS RECOMMENDED THAT YOU BE CLEAR AND RELAXED PRIOR TO DOING THESE EXERCISES. (See Clearing, Relaxation and How to Relax in Chapter 7.)

CREATING INDIVIDUAL RUNS

Here it is important to know which training sessions challenge you, what in particular challenges you in those sessions and which parts and sections of runs and races challenge you.

You need to create supporting mindsets only for areas of your running that you've yet to master. Also be aware of areas in which you might have become stale or resigned to things being as they are. If some part of your running is mediocre, address it. Mediocrity is dull!

Before/during a fartlek/repetition/track/hill session, I repeat the following to myself:

_____

_____

_____

_____

I know that by repeating the appropriate phrases to myself prior to races/hills/repetition training/fartlek/long runs, I feel/experience:

_____

_____

_____

_____

Three-fourths of the way into a race I re-focus my concentration by:

_____

_____

_____

_____

When I am about to commence the last part of a race or tough run I prepare myself by:

_____

_____

_____

_____

When the going gets tough in a race or run, I easily push through by:

_____

_____

_____

_____

The affirmations I use when I stand at the start line are:

_____

_____

_____

_____

The affirmations I use when I run a hilly section are:

_____

_____

_____

_____

The affirmations I use before each run are:

_____

_____

_____

_____

The affirmations I use when I feel tired are:

_____

_____

_____

_____

The affirmations I use when I realize I'm losing concentration are:

_____

_____

_____

_____

NOTES: Other areas that require planned thoughts:

_____

_____

CREATING A LIFETIME OF RUNNING

When I awake for my early morning run I say the following to myself:

_____

_____

_____

_____

Before a demanding training session I say:

_____

_____

_____

_____

When I step up to the start line of a race I tell myself:

_____

_____

_____

_____

When finding time to run is a problem, I tell myself:

_____

_____

_____

_____

When I ponder my life and running I think of:

_____

_____

_____

_____

When I'm asked why I run/love to run, I say:

_____

_____

_____

_____

When I wonder if all the training and discipline are worth it, I believe it when I say:

_____

_____

_____

_____

My fondest running memories are:

_____

_____

_____

_____

_____

_____

_____

_____

_____

_____

_____

FURTHER USEFUL HINTS & EXAMPLES

Questions to ask:

Can you and do you create effective mental strategies that bring you enjoyable and effective training and focused, successful races?

Are you clear on how you want to run your next race?

What are your mental strategies for each phase of the race?

Times that typically require affirmations and planning:

- 48 hours prior to races
- The night before an event
- The 4 hours before an event
- At the start
- During sections that involve uphill running
- When it is hot and/or humid
- Between 75% and 90% into the race (for example, miles 19 to 23, or kilometers 31 to 38 in a marathon)
- To begin a finishing kick early
- Self-praise and acknowledgement after ALL runs

EXAMPLES OF SUBJECTIVE THOUGHTS AND AFFIRMATIONS:

- Keep it simple   *"The race is a journey"*
- Empty mind   *"My mind is quiet"*
- Flow/relax   *"I am at peace"*
- Smooth/excited   *"I draw energy from runners around me"*
- Economical/charged   *"I draw energy from my surroundings"*
- Soft/powerful   *"I am floating"*
- Light/balanced   *"I am a dancer/gymnast"*
- Efficient/harmonious   *"I have rhythmic focus"*

- Dancing feet   *"I am masterful"*
- Joyful/fun   *"I am light and smiling"*
- Satisfying   *"I am relaxed and fulfilled"*
- Enjoying/having fun   *"I let go and let the race happen"*

EXAMPLES OF OBJECTIVE THOUGHTS:

- *Run in the moment*
- *Keep arms close to body*
- *Work with what you have*
- *Use your whole foot when striking the ground*
- *Control*
- *Be calculating*
- *Use your arms*
- *Be what you ask of yourself*
- *"Pitter patter" (a rapid stride cadence)*
- *Breathe*
- *Relax your shoulders and face*

Remember that the easiest way to create a mental strategy is to design it parallel to your physical plan.

EXAMPLE:

When I do hill training, my affirmation is: "I grow more powerful with each repetition session I do."

Then in a race or tough run, when you hit the climbs, your physical strategy might be to use your arms more vigorously, shorten your stride and increase your cadence. With this, your key affirmation might be, "I am trained and skilled and enjoy the hills." Use each training run as an opportunity to design, test and modify your continually growing mental strategy. Break each run or race into phases. Design physical and mental strategies for each phase.

EXAMPLE:

In my next marathon on "x" date I am going to take the following approach:

- Each evening I am going to spend 3 to 5 minutes considering the next day's training and the affirmations I am going to use at certain points in the session. I am going to visualize the workout in detail and experience how successful it is.

- On the way to each session I am going to clear my mind by using a clearing exercise (Chapter 7), and I am going to recall some of my most successful training sessions. At the outset of each training run I choose that it be a wonderful experience, and I ensure that it is. After each session I say to myself that one more piece of the plan is securely in place.

- 3 days prior to the race I confirm regularly to myself that I am ready. I ensure that all physical details are handled (shoes, transport, meals, accommodation, racing gear, etc.). I praise and congratulate myself for my thoroughness and professional approach. I enjoy the feeling of readiness and eagerness. I look forward to race day. I am fit, ready and excited. I have stated how I intend to be during the race. I have told those whom I trust and love what my targets are and have shared with them all other intentions that I have.

- On race day my affirmations inspire me with confidence. I am relaxed and calm. My preparation and planning leave nothing to chance.

- At the start (of the marathon): I rapidly establish a good rhythm. My thoughts are subjective and my mood words are ... (See "subjective thoughts.") I am in control.

- In the next segment say from 6 to 13 miles, (10 to 21K): I have great form. I establish my own pace. I am patient and wise. I am having fun.

- From 13 to 18 miles, (21 to 29K): My strength training starts to pay off. My form is excellent. I continue to create my race. I hydrate well.

- From 18 to 23 miles, (29 to 37K): I constantly affirm myself. I notice my self-talk and concentrate on my commitment. I'm strong and I embrace discomfort, knowing it indicates excellence. I recognize the good/power in every situation. My training empowers me. I hold my form. I relax. (See "objective thoughts.")

- The final section: I'm free to give my all. I'm excited by how good I feel. I stay focused. The finish line draws me toward it. I feel how well I've run. I relish the moment.

Each run is best planned by:

- Choosing specific affirmations for specific sections
  EXAMPLES: *"I'm prepared"*
  "I'm willing"
  "I love it"

- Giving yourself clear and specific instructions
  EXAMPLES: *"Show good form"*
  "Use your strong arms"
  "Be light on your feet"

- Pre-setting an effective mood
  EXAMPLES: *"I look great"*
  "I feel great"
  "I am great"

- Creating the correct mindset
  EXAMPLES: *"I'm ready"*
  "I deal with circumstances"
  "I can handle this"
  "I was born for this"

HOW ARE YOU DOING WITH CHAPTER 9
PLANNING THE PERFECT RUNNING EXPERIENCE

Record the date each time you focus on this component

Date	Date	Date	Date

How do you rate your proficiency with this component?
(Write a date and a score out of five in the block next to the date.)

Rating Scale: 5 = excellent, 4 = good, 3 = acceptable, 2 = poor, 1 = very poor

Date	Score	Date	Score	Date	Score	Date	Score	4 week av.

Comments (Periodically write down any realizations you have in this area. How does having a mental strategy eliminate the risk of a mediocre or unsuccessful running experience?)

Date
_____

Date
_____

Date
_____

CHOICES TO RUN BY
MAKING THE BEST CHOICES FOR YOUR RUNNING

"The last of the human freedoms—to choose one's
attitude in any given set of circumstances, to choose ones way"
- VIKTOR FRANKL

The word responsible, when broken into its elements, is "response able", or "able to respond." To really understand the power of choice, you need to fully accept that you have a choice, no matter what the circumstances. In fact everything in your life is the way it is because of choices you make. In other words, you are responsible.

PROACTIVE OR REACTIVE RUNNING?

When it comes to choices, there are two types of runners, proactive and reactive.

Reactive runners—these are people who wait for others to do something first before they react, for example, "I cannot train properly for a marathon until my wife gets a job." Reactive people do not initiate. They allow circumstances to rule their lives. If nothing causes them to react, nothing happens. "I'll never get fit until this weather lets up and I can train."

Pro-active runners—these are people who act when they decide that action is necessary, for example, "He's ahead of me, I'll need to accelerate in order to pass him effectively." Pro-active people make life happen; they create opportunities for themselves; they succeed or take steps in the direction of success and always act. Such people are happy, effective, creative, responsible and successful. They do not "try," they either "do" or "do not do." They consider both success and failure as steps toward victory and "trying" as pointless-the only real failure.

"This is real freedom—the ability to enjoy the choices we make in every successive moment of the present. It is the ability to spontaneously put our attention on those choices that brings joy to us and also to others."

- DEEPAK CHOPRA

THE DANGERS OF "TRYING" AS OPPOSED TO "DOING"

"Trying" is often a way of not being responsible. Society rewards "trying your best." But notice how you avoid the lessons failure can teach when you dismiss an outcome simply by saying: "I tried." There is nothing wrong with attempting a difficult running challenge and failing. What is problematic for runners is when they start out on a difficult quest with the notion that they can avoid facing up to the implications (and therefore gaining any value!) of failure by appeasing themselves and others by saying they tried. It is far better to go for success and fully accept failure as one more step in the journey to success. In other words, reward your own success and failure equally, as functions of attempting with the purpose to succeed, not to appease your own ego or satisfy a societal demand to have tried your best.

You can therefore either choose TO DO (proactive) or have DONE (reactive) to you.

THE SPACE BETWEEN STIMULUS AND RESPONSE

There is a space between a stimulus and your response to it. When something happens (a stimulus), there is always an opportunity in which to decide what the best action (response) should be. Often a behavior is so regularly repeated that one does not even realize this—that you have a choice in your reaction. If you've run one particular race badly two years in a row, you might have unconsciously chosen to believe you are not good at this event. Subsequently you have a defeatist attitude even before you race. If you realize that this is a choice you have made, you can remake the choice by saying, "I choose to believe that (this time) I master this race". Deal only with what is there on the day, and choose not to carry the past into the event.

If your "automatic" reactions do not have the desired outcome, and they do not serve you or your purposes, you need to choose other, more effective responses. Through drills and training you can repeatedly choose new, powerful responses that work, until they too become automatic.

SEEK THE OPPORTUNITIES THAT STIMULI PROVIDE

Remember, we cannot change behavior by adapting a mindset that says, "don't do that" because the mind cannot "not" do—it can only "do."

For example, if we tell ourselves not to go out too fast, we access a well-practiced program in our minds that ensures that we do go out too fast! Instead, we need to choose a response that says in the affirmative, "Go out smoothly, at a controlled and relaxed even pace." This will bring about the desired result. (See Chapter 7.)

The way to solve the challenge of continually attempting to alter or change ineffectual behaviors can be miraculously met by replacing old, ineffectual behaviors with new, effective ones. (For more information on this skill, see Chapter 7 also.)

For example, in the past you used to believe you could not deal with an uneven pace. Now you know you can and have trained to be able to do so. You respond to an uneven pace during a group run by choosing a new response that says: "I love running at an uneven pace, because it gives me a chance to test my fitness and my resolve. If the pace is uneven, I will be ready."

Certain choices seem particularly daunting. When you seem to be having no luck with your choices in an area, consider whether you are taking on the correct challenge. Specifically, remember that you have no control over outcomes or results. How long have coaches and runners attempted to predict times, only to be foiled by circumstances like the weather? You can only choose your responses and subsequent attitude. Choose processes, actions and how you want to be, rather than outcomes (see Chapters 4 and 5).

Read how Steve Scott described the day he made the choice that changed his running career and life forever:

"The biggest incident in my life that helped me to achieve a passion for running occurred back in 1976. I was just finishing my sophomore year at Irvine. I didn't make it through the first round of the NCAA. I placed in the AAU meet, but didn't have an Olympic Trials qualifying mark. The Trials needed 36 runners to fill the field, and they only had 33 that had the standard. My coach made a strong pitch that I be allowed to compete in the Trials even though I was 5th in line. His argument was that I was young and needed the experience for the future. What he failed to tell this committee was that I was the biggest goof-off athletics had ever seen. I always finished the workouts that the coach gave us as long as he was standing over me. I was also known to cut a workout short by jumping on the back of the van coach was driving, as a way of escaping the interval we would run on the road.

"However, my coach prevailed and I was allowed to compete in the Olympic Trials. To the amazement of many people, including myself, I made it through the first round, past the semi-finals and into the finals. In the finals I achieved a 7th place, falling well short of making it into the Olympics.

"The real eye-opener happened the next morning when I left my dorm room to get some breakfast. I was met by about a half a dozen athletes who had run in different events the day before preparing to go for a run. I was astonished at the fact that they were running after the events of the night before. It was my practice to take the day off after a meet. They shared with me the fact that they run every day and sometimes twice a day, and on this particular day, they were going to run 15 miles.

"Well, something inside me just clicked. I asked myself, 'If I made it to the Olympic Trials finals with my lack of dedication, effort and sincerity, what would happen if I had the same passion and attitude that these other athletes possessed?' From that point on, I made serious changes in my approach to running both physically and mentally, and they paid off immediately! The next season, the spring of 1977, I won the National Championships in the 1,500-meters, was ranked # 1 in the country and # 9 in the world.

"The key to success is having a passion for what you do. When you have passion, even the most difficult task will be enjoyable. From 1977 on, I was able to take the work out of a workout."

Along with Jim Ryan, Steve Scott is arguably the best miler (3:46), to come out of the United States, competing successfully in his heyday with the likes of Sebastian Coe and Said Aouita.

ATTACH TO ATTITUDES, NOT OUTCOMES

In her build-up to the Berlin marathon in 1996, Colleen De Reuck focused on being a world-class marathon runner. She accepted that she had trained like one and went to the start line adamant that she was not "racing" against anyone other than herself. She had won many shorter distance races and was up against the belief that she had not fully realized her potential as a marathon runner. We decided that the perfect result to the race would be to have her say afterward that she had managed to give a full account of her training and had run as hard as she could. A personal best and a world-class time would be secondary bonuses.

She went on to win the race in a personal best time, but the overriding impression she was left with after the race was one of satisfaction at being able to utilize her attitude during the run and not have her attention on time or opponents. It makes sense that if you are able to concentrate fully and objectively on getting all you have out of yourself during a run, there will be no regrets regarding the outcome.

Great attachment to certain outcomes can only ultimately lead to embarrassment and bitter disappointment. Saying "If I don't run under 50-minutes for 10K today I'm going to quit this stupid sport" is self-sabotaging. Instead choose statements about attitudes and behaviors that you do have control over and can commit to, such as: "I choose to be patient and dedicated while unswervingly pursuing my targets." This leads to the reward of being patient and dedicated. They are both wonderful traits to know you have and to be remembered by, even if you do not achieve some of your targets. After all, it is the striving that represents a runner's life, not the outcome. These are but milestones along the way. The way IS the thing!

When faced with choices, first determine whether the issue represents something over which you are concerned, but have no influence, or whether you can actually do something about the matter. Being worried about whether the wind is going to influence your performance or not is an unnessessary concern. If however you are deciding whether you should grab a race drink at this aid station or the next, then there is something you can do that could influence your performance.

Considering and acting only on areas where we have recourse, power or influence greatly reduces stress levels when faced with a multiplicity of choices. Don't bother with those situations about which you can do nothing!

Determine whether you have any influence over a situation before you agonize over it. Make choices that serve you, your running, and the sport. Always be aware that you have a choice and that you have time to choose before you act. You can act more effectively if you have considered your choices beforehand.

There are few better writers on the subject of running than Runner's World editor Amby Burfoot, himself a world-class runner in his day. To him his choice was to move from being an elite runner to being a life-time runner, here's why:

"For me, running is one of the best and healthiest of activities precisely because it offers so many choices. I can run slow or fast, alone or in a group, short or long, in daylight or in darkness, in heat waves or blizzards, on trails or roads or tracks or beaches.

"The list is nearly endless. Indeed, it's as long as the individual runner's ability to be creative. To choose is to create. I like that part of running too.

"When I was young, I chose to run as fast as I could. At the time—please forgive me—I didn't know any better. I thought running was about winning, or at least trying to win. I was lucky enough to win a few races, including the Boston marathon, and this reinforced my decision to run as fast as possible.

"I pushed harder and harder and harder. This is what all elite athletes do, of course, and we ask no sympathy. We wouldn't push so hard if we didn't enjoy occasional successes. We wouldn't push so hard if we didn't feel the allure of laurel wreaths. I ran fast, and I was happy that I could beat the other runners in my race.

"Of course, this doesn't last for long. The fast runner must eventually get older and slower, and I did. This is precisely the time that tries men's soles. Should I just quit entirely? The outsider might argue: Yes. Running provides few material rewards, after all, and none for the slow runner.

"But the true runner never quits, because he doesn't measure running in terms of material rewards. The rewards of running are all immaterial. They are choices. I choose to continue running because it makes me feel better everyday. It gives me energy and mental focus. It takes me places, both in the physical world and the psychological world, where I have never gone before.

"Not to run would be to stagnate. Instead, I choose to run in ways I have never run before. I run slower than ever, that's for sure. I don't time myself very often. I run with my wife (she used to be too slow for me, but not any more), I run with my teenage children (an exciting new experience), I lead marathon-pacing groups where we run together as a team with a shared goal time (4 hours). I cross-train more. But that doesn't make me less of a runner. I always return to running as my primary fitness activity. I even do workouts where I alternate running and walking. Walking? Sure. I've found that the run-walk method feels good, prevents injuries, and helps me extend the length of my workouts.

"Choices? There are thousands of them, and everyone's a winner; as long as you make the choice to stay active."

"I MAKE THE RIGHT CHOICES"

"I CHOOSE MY STATE OF MIND"

BECOMING AWARE OF YOUR RUNNING CHOICES

IT IS RECOMMENDED THAT YOU BE CLEAR AND RELAXED PRIOR TO THESE EXERCISES. (See Clearing, Relaxation and How to Relax in Chapter 7.)

State the types of choices and/or specific choices you typically need to make before specific sessions or races, (include the choices you would make):

_____

_____

_____

_____

_____

_____

_____

_____

_____

EXAMPLE:

Predicament: *"I really dread these Wednesday group runs. I get so tired after 45 minutes and have to hang on for dear life over the last quarter of an hour."*

Choice: *"I will communicate this to the group. I choose to run with the second group. Their pace suits me and will serve me better. In time I could graduate to the next pace up again."*

State the universal or regular choices you always seem to have around your running. These are your running career questions. Remember the more you consider these when you are calm, logical, fresh, relaxed and in control of the situation, the greater the likelihood that they will be less daunting when they are thrust upon you. By pre-determining the choices you have and carefully selecting possible responses, you significantly reduce the amount of time it takes to choose in the heat of the moment. Your responses are also more informed and considered.

_____

_____

_____

_____

_____

_____

_____

_____

EXAMPLE:

Stimulus: *"Whenever I race against so-and-so I seem to have a bad race."*

Response: *"I've created this race on every level. He/she has no influence on my performance. When thoughts of him/her arise in my mind, I simply allow them to be there. I do not judge them. I allow them to pass and see them fade powerlessly."*

FURTHER USEFUL HINTS & EXAMPLES

Questions to ask yourself:

Are you in constant, happy control of your running and your racing?

If you are not in control, why are you not?

By when will you be?

What actions do you need to take to regain the control you want?

Are you choosing powerfully and effectively when faced with choices for your running?

Are you recognizing the space between stimulus and response in which you get to choose?

Are you choosing appropriate responses that serve you?

Are you taking responsibility for your actions and responses regarding your running?

What are you unnecessarily concerned about in your running?

Are you exercising the influence you have over your running?

HOW ARE YOU DOING WITH CHAPTER 10?
MAKING THE BEST CHOICES FOR YOUR RUNNING

Record the date each time you focus on this component

Date	Date	Date	Date

How do you rate your proficiency with this component?
(Write a date and a score out of five in the block next to the date.)

Rating Scale: 5 = excellent, 4 = good, 3 = acceptable, 2 = poor, 1 = very poor

Date	Score	Date	Score	Date	Score	Date	Scor	4 week av.

Comments (Periodically write down any realizations you have in this area. How does knowing that you have a choice in everything actually give you power if you are willing to take on responsibility?)

Date

_____

Date

_____

Date

_____

RUNNING UNCHALLENGED
MEETING RUNNING CHALLENGES

"Problems are those fearful things we
see when we take our eyes off our goals."
- ANONYMOUS

You grow by taking on the challenges that a life of running provides. Once you make this point a creed by which you live, your running becomes an adventure and not a constant effort to avoid problems. The whole of life consists of moving forward by accepting greater and greater challenges. With the right attitude all challenges are an opportunity to learn and progress, even if you feel you are not always succeeding. You still grow by the lessons you learn (Chapter 10).

Sometimes the challenges that you face in your running life are far greater than just how to achieve lifetime bests. Priscilla Welch provides a dramatic example:

"As time marched on, I got too focused and wrapped up in my own career, although I could feel subtle changes going on which puzzled me. I became too tunnel-visioned. Life had to bring me back to reality. I had to be forcibly taught to respect my body more throughout hormonal changes. In 1992 I discovered that I had breast cancer, which shockingly told me and others that we are still very vulnerable even if we eat right and exercise right. But being very fit at the onset enabled me to overcome and continue on with life—this time with much wider vision and a lot more respect for my body and compassion for others. I became a member of a huge club where the subscription is the (answer to the) question: 'Are you a survivor?'

"Life is after all a series of tests; you either pass or not. It's essential though that one should keep the body exercised in order to keep the brain and body in balance, so coping with whatever comes our way next can be dealt with, no matter the outcome."

Priscilla attributes her recovery from this debilitating disease to the mental toughness she gained from running and her strength from being running-fit at the time.

INTERPRETATION VS. FACT

Interpretation varies from one runner to the next. I coach a runner who is afraid to ride down a steep rocky trail on a mountain bike, but fears nothing when lining up against the world's best with 85,000 runners behind her and winning the race! It is not any given situation that is stressful, but our interpretation of it.

Get into the habit of questioning your interpretations. Then make new choices about your negative interpretations. You'll find that you will be able to reduce stress and pressure with your new choices. Three days before Josia Thugwane won the Olympic marathon in Atlanta, I was speaking to him and one of the other South African competitors. I asked whom they were concerned about in the race. The other runner replied that their chances of doing well were slim, as the very best in the world (based on best times) were in the race. Josia's interpretation was as follows: "I do not know who is in the race, and it does not matter. The runners I must race against will be at my shoulder when the real racing begins." Wise words indeed, and a realistic interpretation of what was to be expected in the race.

"Problems" actually exist only in language. What we say is what we have interpreted. The cold only becomes a problem in a race to those who say to themselves or others that the cold is going to be a problem. For an animal there are no problems. A situation is as it is and the animal deals with this. If an antelope is hungry, it does what it can to eat. If food is in short supply and it fails on a given day, it simply continues with its life and its search for food. There is no interpretation, only an acceptance of the facts. There is much peace to be had by following the behavior of the antelope.

QUESTION YOUR INTERPRETATIONS

For runners, real power lies in analyzing why you have interpreted certain situations in certain ways. By constantly ensuring that you interpret a situation for what it is, objectively, you gain control and access to effective responses.

A runner whom I coach had struggled for years to break the 30-minute barrier for 10K. He had all the shorter-distance credentials to prove that he could achieve such a performance. Ability was not the problem. So I asked him which specific workouts he had done in the past which best indicate his fitness to him. He said that the session that gave him the most confidence was a series of one-kilometer repeats on the track. We arranged to meet at the track in a few days. I reminded him of his best and average session of this nature. Just before he started I asked him to give me his stopwatch. He was not very eager to do this (as many runners would react), but handed me the watch anyway.

I then proceeded to time the session and ask him what times he thought he was doing. He consistently underestimated his time. He ran progressively faster and faster until I stopped the session because he had started to slow down.

Without telling him the times, I assured him he was in shape to achieve his target of sub-30 minutes. I also asked him not to wear a watch in the race. The instructions I gave him were simple: "Go out with the leaders and deal with whatever comes up." He proceeded to run 29:45, some 45-seconds faster than his best!

His achievement was due to not having had access to information from which he could make an assumption (interpretation). He ran based on trust and feel. He had to trust me that he was fit enough, and he had to listen to his body regarding the pace he could deal with. The information he had previously was always interpreted from the stopwatch and was not relevant. Yet he had allowed it to determine how well he could run.

Learn to question your interpretations. Do not necessarily act upon them as if they are the truth.

STRESS AS AN INTERPRETATION

Stress does not really exist; it is an interpretation of a given situation as stressful. The concept of creating pressure for yourself does exist. "Stress" is at its most damaging when you believe that it is something that is being forced upon you. Accept that you progress by taking on and creating manageable stress in your life.

You grow through stress. For example, you gradually and progressively stress your mind and body to deal with more and more training until you can complete a 10K. Then with more mental and physical stress (training) you can do a half-marathon. All this manageable stress is termed *Eustress* (good for us).

If however you attempted to run a marathon on 2 weeks of running 10 miles (16 kilometers) a week, that would be *Distress*. Your body would break down in the race. You would lose confidence and no longer have the belief that you could do it.

Just as you would do with training, you need to gradually take on more and more challenging mental situations. In this way you become mentally tough.

Without this you do not grow as a runner, or human being for that matter. The secret is to have the insight to not get in over your head, but to control and effectively interpret each challenge and stressful situation so that you grow progressively and do not break down and have to begin again.

PROBLEMS AS OPPORTUNITIES

All problems are opportunities. You must acquire the presence of mind to always realize this. Seek until you discover what that opportunity is. Often it will require a leap of faith, as the value of the challenge might not be immediately recognizable or available. There will always be value. By knowing and believing this you gain strength, courage and the ability to take on all the challenges your running presents.

Johnny Halberstadt, famous South African runner and successful running business man, speaks of his years in apartheid South Africa as opportunity:

(As a result of South Africa's discriminatory policy that disallowed equal rights, the world imposed various boycotts upon the country. This was to pressure the government into accepting democratic rule. One of these embargos prevented any South African from participating in international sport.)

"In retrospect experiencing my running career as a South African in the height of the apartheid sports boycott era was probably more fulfilling and action-packed that it would ever have been under any other circumstances. Sure it was tough not being able to go to the Olympics, but living every day on the cutting edge of tumultuous change was dramatic, exciting, exhilarating, scary, challenging, unforgettable. The good times, friendships, heartaches, terror, jubilation, and every emotion one can experience, packed into a short space of time is something I will always treasure and be grateful for. When you are thrust into the public eye, you find yourself put into the position of having to explore the depths of your very soul to find out who you really are.

"Circumstances allowed me to become one of the first modern day full-time athletes in South Africa to earn a living from running-related income only. With an MBA-degree it could have been easy to chase the money and disappear into a much 'safer' run-of-the-mill type of existence, but following my running passion has enriched me in ways no other lifestyle could."

Johnny, who studied with a scholarship at Oklahoma State, is one of an elite group of runners who has run 2:12 for the marathon and broken 4-minutes for the mile. He runs two highly successful running stores in Colorado.

It is essential to see challenges as a normal phenomenon.

To expect that everything will always go according to plan, smoothly and predictably, is unrealistic. If you choose to believe that your running should always be hassle free, you are setting yourself up for disappointment. If this is your attitude, all setbacks will only lead to a loss of confidence and motivation. Growth can only occur through the meeting of challenges. The next time a tough problem stares you in the face, relish the prospect of a good challenge and apply the following principles.

7-STEPS TO EFFECTIVELY MEET CHALLENGES

1. State what you committed yourself to in your running.

2. Decide what kind of runner would experience this kind of problem.

3. Establish why YOU consider the situation to be a problem.

4. Determine what kind of runner would rapidly solve this situation and then become that runner.

5. Act in a way that will alleviate the problem. For example, be objective, maintain a sense of humor, and avoid complaining and excuses.

6. Stop blaming yourself or others for the situation. Forgive yourself and others. Rather praise and accept others.

7. Act! Do something positive, constructive and creative. Do it with confidence. Any action creates movement. Doing nothing creates nothing.

By following these guidelines, even if the first attempts are unsuccessful, a solution usually appears. This holds true for training, racing and all the other factors and activities that constitute your running experience.

This planned and practiced approach to mastering challenges will provide rapid and less exhausting solutions. Have these questions and their relevant answers form part of the key to meeting all your running challenges.

Design an affirmation that comes to mind whenever you are challenged, for example, "When challenged I apply the 7-steps." Just knowing you have this ability will provide confidence and security.

FEAR

Your only fear is the fear of the unknown. No situation contains fear. You bring fear into a situation. Prior to the Barcelona Olympic 10,000-meter men's heats I told a prominent South African runner that he had nothing to fear about running 25 laps around a 400-meter track, as he had done it better than any South African had ever done, for a good many years. He realized that there was nothing within the race to fear, and that he had created the fear himself. As soon as he focused upon the race and his ability, he was able to dispel his fear and get on with what he does best. He qualified for the final.

Not knowing or being able to control what might occur next in any new or challenging situation can be termed "fear." In order to get past this interpretation, accept that you cannot predict the future. Give your problem fixed parameters by laying it out in full. Once it is out in the open, apply the 7-steps. By accepting that you will be challenged and by having a method by which you approach these challenges, fear is diminished. You now know that "stuff" happens and also know what to do when this "stuff" occurs, even if you don't know what will happen.

This knowledge provides you with control. With control come peace and calm. With peace and calm comes clarity. With clarity comes appropriate action, and with appropriate action come solutions, resolution and recourse. You now have insight into the nature of progress. From this you can grow, all the while gaining satisfaction, self-esteem and self-realization through your running.

"I CREATE SOLUTIONS FOR MY RUNNING "

THE JOY OF DISCOMFORT

With competitive runners, a large part of distance running success is about dealing effectively with the physiological discomfort of exertion on a mental level. There is much to be learned from the top runner in this regard.

Once again it's all about interpretation. Messages sent from working muscles indicate only an intensity of work being performed. Some runners interpret this as pain (a non-runner running to catch a train that is about to leave), or discomfort (an inexperienced runner attempting a distance beyond his or her current experience), while other runners interpret this as enjoyment (a well-conditioned runner pushing the pace in a race).

Some interesting research has shown that people with a particular ability to "endure" are the ones drawn to running and other endurance sports. It is obvious in discussions with non-runners that they really don't understand what it is runners see in running! They see it only as uncomfortable, pointless and painful!

THE VALUE OF PAIN

Some of this is tied up in the value of discomfort or pain. Philosophers have pondered the possibility that the only way to grow is through the endurance of pain. Hence the old slogan in physical exercise of "no pain, no gain." If you think about it, much of how you live is entirely determined by either an avoidance of pain or a search for pleasure.

No matter what your level of running, improvement or growth comes about only as a result of moving beyond the comfort zone—and this involves some discomfort. Many people have been sadly lost to this glorious sport because they went unguided into their first running endeavor and experienced such discomfort that they were scared off for life! This could have happened at school with an insensitive coach, teacher or parent. It could have happened during an experience with a well-meaning but uninformed friend who was either much fitter or much more talented. Suffice to say that your initial steps in running very powerfully shape how you relate to the sport from that point on.

If you are reading this, you are no doubt a committed runner already. Knowing how to effectively negotiate the very real physical barriers that running presents will have a beneficial effect on your future running experiences. Be aware of your choice of words and actions when you introduce others to the sport in the future.

Success in competitive distance running requires a finely developed ability to deal with discomfort. To make satisfactory gains in fitness also requires breaking through discomfort barriers. In order to attain these gains, there are two distinct areas that require attention.

DEALING WITH THE DISCOMFORT

It is essential to have a clear understanding of the physiological mechanisms that create discomfort through exertion in running. This understanding provides you with the ability to factually interpret the nature of the discomfort produced by running hard. In this way the "monster" of pain that strikes fear into the heart of the mentally unprepared runner, to you simply becomes a logical physiological phenomenon that indicates an intense level of physical exertion. When others believe themselves to be tired, you know that your experience can either be translated as a defeating tiredness like theirs or can be used as a further step toward achieving greatness in your running.

Once you know you have the choice of either "exhaustion" or "challenge," the answer becomes clear, meet the challenge!

THE PHYSIOLOGY OF PAIN

Running is not created in the brain, as a picture would be when you paint, for example. Running, as stated before, is a reflex action that occurs in your spinal column. Decisions to accelerate, jump, slow down or stop are formed in the brain.

The "pain" experienced from muscle fatigue during hard running occurs when neural (nerve) receptors at the site of the working muscles, in the blood, lungs and heart send a message that indicates you are moving toward the edges of the limits your body deems safe. This is part of the body's natural tendency to remain within or return to these limits and is called homeostasis.

A healthy functioning body cannot exceed these limits naturally, so you are perfectly safe. Your body will signal your brain to slow down or stop, should matters get "out-of-hand." Training teaches you that these limits are not as rigid or fixed as your brain initially "told" you (an interpretation). You can take on more and more discomfort as you recognize the discomfort for what it is, then apply your strategies and stick to your commitments with passion and discipline.

Elite distance runners interpret discomfort with a much higher pain threshold. Through intense training they constantly meet these acute pain levels and reinterpret them to develop coping strategies that allow them to endure far greater levels of discomfort for longer periods of time—higher even than physiologists initially deemed possible. Every new season athletes push back the so-called limits of human endeavor, proving that the mind is more the limit to feats of greatness than the body.

There are two downsides to this scenario against which you should guard:

- When you are ill, especially with a fever or other viral infection, and insist on training, you override these protection devices and can do permanent damage, or even kill yourself.

- Drugs, especially stimulants, mask your ability to accurately sense, monitor and evaluate discomfort. By using these you can push beyond your true limits and either kill yourself or do permanent damage.

IMPORTANT
Don't train when you are ill and don't mess with so-called
performance-enhancing drugs.

DISCOMFORT IS VOLUNTARY

Remind yourself that you are voluntarily subjecting yourself to this pain and can, should you so choose, stop or slow down and the feeling will diminish and disappear. This is a very powerful realization. You create the circumstances for the discomfort in the full knowledge of its depth and intensity. This gives you the power of knowing that this is what you want and are therefore perfectly willing and able to deal with it.

- **Embrace the discomfort:** Welcoming the pain is the clearest indication that you are seeking performance and honoring your commitment to excellence by giving of your best. Percy Cerutty, the great Australian distance coach of the 1950's, said, "Embrace pain like a lover" for this very reason.

- **Be prepared:** Plan a strategy (Chapter 9). Through visualizing (Chapter 7) and experiencing how you might feel (Chapter 8) and then recognizing the onset of discomfort, you can use pre-planned affirmations (Chapter 2) to effectively harness your experience to further you along your journey of performance and self-discovery.

- **Look forward to the experience:** Look forward to the onset of this experience, for it is an opportunity to further your aims (Chapters 4 and 5).

- **Recognize your awareness and control:** Praise yourself for having been logically aware and in control of the situation. Evaluate your success and if necessary modify your strategy for the next experience.

APPRECIATING THE DISCOMFORT

This might sound rather masochistic at first, but bear with me, it will soon become clear. You only truly discover who you are when your confrontation with pain presents you with distinct possibilities. You transcend pain when you cease to question the origin or judge its validity or identity in your life.

For example, you have decided that you are fit and know before a race that you are ready. The weather and other conditions are perfect. The pace is right. You have no excuses. All that remains to be done is to deal with each doubt, each fear, each challenge, each bad patch as it arises—no more, no less. Recognize that the pain is self-induced. Welcome it as a clear indication of performance. Relish your power and control over this discomfort.

If you do not put yourself into positions where you are under pressure and require of yourself to choose to deal with whatever arises, you will never have the opportunity to know your own greatness.

You can only grow through continually dealing with discomfort. Anything else is nothing more than stagnation.

Whether you "win" or "lose" any given battle with the challenges you place before yourself through your running is irrelevant. What is of life-affirming importance is that you never cease from taking on these challenges; always higher, greater, further—onward and upward.

SOLVING YOUR RUNNING CHALLENGES

IT IS RECOMMENDED THAT YOU BE CLEAR AND RELAXED PRIOR TO THESE EXERCISES. (See Clearing, Relaxation and How to Relax in Chapter 7.)

Choose a typical challenge that arises in your running and work through it with the 7-step model. (See page 182.)

Challenge:

EXAMPLE: *I'm afraid of very short races: They involve so much pain.*

_____

_____

_____

Step 1. What did you commit yourself to in your running?

_____

_____

_____

_____

EXAMPLE: *I am committed to being the best I can be and short races provide great opportunities to develop and test my discomfort management strategies.*

Step 2. What kind of runner would experience this kind of problem?

_____

_____

_____

EXAMPLE: *One who is disempowered, out of control, scared, helpless and unwilling to grow.*

Step 3. Why do you consider the situation to be a problem?

_____

_____

_____

EXAMPLE: *I don't like short races, because they hurt and I do poorly.*

Step 4. What kind of runner would rapidly solve this situation? Become that runner.

_____

_____

_____

EXAMPLE: *I runner who is prepared and excited. A runner who feels confident and capable. A runner who has a physical and mental strategy. A runner who relishes a challenge and who realizes the greater the challenge the greater the breakthrough. A runner who finds and creates solutions.*

Step 5. Act in a way that will alleviate the problem.

_____

_____

_____

EXAMPLE: *Instead of complaining and hesitating, I'm just going to do it. I'm going to make a point of only saying positive things about this opportunity. I'm going to apologize to those people I whined to about it. I will praise myself and find the good in it all, instead of making excuses before or after. I look forward to the event.*

Step 6. Stop blaming yourself or others for the situation. Forgive yourself and others. Praise and accept others.

_____

_____

_____

EXAMPLE: *It's not my friend's fault for entering me in the race. I choose to run it. It's not anybody's fault. I am fit and well prepared. Blaming myself for not preparing correctly is not only a waste of time, but will prove detrimental as a racing mindset. I am and will be positive throughout this experience. I forgive myself for behaving this way.*

Step 7. Act! Do something positive, constructive and creative. Do it with confidence.

_____

_____

_____

EXAMPLES: *I run hard and with an open mind. I affirm powerfully before and during the event. I analyze the run objectively. I keep the good and let go of the bad. I praise myself and speak excitedly of the experience. I seek wise assistance in preparing for the event.*

FURTHER USEFUL HINTS & EXAMPLES
Questions to ask yourself:

Running is challenging, through it we either grow or break down. Do you have an effective strategy to meet the challenges?

Are you powerfully meeting the challenges that arise?

Say to yourself, "I have something of (great) value to learn here. Perhaps I'll not instantly recognize that, but every challenge that is placed before me is an opportunity. I'll accept each challenge as an opportunity to grow and nothing more."

If this running challenge seems impossible to overcome, ask yourself what kind of a runner you are that cannot solve this problem. Are you impatient? Do you lack confidence? Are you afraid? If so, imagine the kind of runner who would either overcome this challenge or even not see it as a problem in the first place. What characteristics would such a runner have and display?

The traits of people who effectively meet challenges are:
- they are patient
- they are confident
- they relish a challenge
- they are calm
- they make clear choices
- they take responsibility
- they seek opportunities for growth
- they set no limits on themselves
- they have a sense of humor
- they view challenges as opportunities for fun
- they are in action

Take these for yourself; become them and in so doing become the runner who overcomes what you initially thought to be a problem.

HOW ARE YOU DOING WITH CHAPTER 11?
MEETING RUNNING CHALLENGES

Record the date each time you focus on this component

Date	Date	Date	Date

How do you rate your proficiency with this component?
(Write a date and a score out of five in the block next to the date.)

Rating Scale: 5 = excellent, 4 = good, 3 = acceptable, 2 = poor, 1 = very poor

Date	Score	Date	Score	Date	Score	Date	Score	4 week av.

Comments (Periodically write down any realizations you have in this area. How does looking for the value or lesson in each challenge alter how you view your "problems?")

Date

Date

Date

RUNNING AS A GIFT
SHARING YOUR RUNNING

"Life's most persistent and urgent question is:
What are you doing for others?"
- MARTIN LUTHER KING, JR.

WHY DO YOU RUN?

There are many reasons why people run. Once involved in the sport, though, most runners seldom think about why they are doing it. Of course there are times—when the season gets long and pressure increases, or things seem like they are not going as well as they should—when you might find yourself wondering if it is all worth it. It then becomes increasingly valuable to give some attention to why you participate in this wonderful sport of running.

By reaffirming why you run, in great and colorful detail, especially when you experience dark and trying times, you ensure that you rediscover the inspiration and motivation that excited and drew you to running in the first place.

THE SELFISH MINDSET

We all desire to be part of something successful and creative. There are many reasons for personal fulfillment (Chapter 13). When your participation in running feels like something you do only for personal gain, for reasons that seem selfish, like winning or racing for money or prestige, it can begin to feel empty, unfulfilling and anti-climatic. But this needn't be the case.

REALIZE THAT YOU CAN CONTRIBUTE JOY, PLEASURE AND FULFILLMENT TO MANY OTHERS THROUGH YOUR RUNNING.

By running, you are fulfilling a valuable role in your life. Younger runners and fellow competitors look up to you for inspiration. Less capable runners view you as a role model and strive to be like you. Family and friends are proud of you and are inspired by your running. You provide them with something they need: An example that allows them to get in touch with their own needs for self-expression. You give them opportunities to be excited, passionate, patriotic and supportive.

SERVING YOURSELF AND OTHERS THROUGH RUNNING

One of the most important concepts to grasp in the entirety of this book is the following:

The purpose of life, and therefore running is to serve.

Service can be defined as using your life and your running for your own good and the greater good of society in general. This "society" can include friends and family, your immediate community and the world at large.

In the final analysis, your life is most complete and fulfilled when you serve others through your endeavors. In order to do so, however, you first need to be whole and complete, fulfilled and at peace with where you are in your own pursuits. This means you must first serve your own needs, with regard to running and otherwise.

To feel this way you need to nurture your running and feel served in this regard. Once you are emotionally satisfied, whole and complete, and your running is growing in an unrestricted manner, you can powerfully serve others.

Zola Pieterse (previously Zola Budd), was a child prodigy in long distance running, who as a young woman went on to set many world records despite a tragic career marred by unfortunate incidents and politics. A lesser person would have wilted under the immense pressure she found herself under, without any significant emotional support at that time. The fact that she still runs competitively as a mother of three in her mid-30's, and has a wonderful outlook on life, is a tribute to her mental tenacity and balanced outlook. It is worth looking at how she discovered, as a young girl, how her running could serve her, before she went on to serve the running communities of the world.

"I made my first breakthrough in athletics (track) as a 15 year-old girl running barefoot in Bloemfontein, (a city in the South African hinterland).

"The build up to the race was very strenuous to me, because another local girl was the favorite and I was under a lot of pressure to beat her. My previous best time for the 1,500-meters was approximately 4:20 (about 4:39 for the mile). I can still remember the last 10 minutes before the race. I was overwhelmed by all the pressure and my legs felt like elephant stilts! When I looked at my coach at the side of the track, my stomach sounded like my mom's washing machine. When I looked at my opponents, death looked more inviting. I had totally lost it, and I knew it.

"Out of pure desperation, I turned my back on it all and walked down the track, away from the start. In that silence I saw the day turn purple-orange in the west and the smell of the evening filled my senses. The track felt cool and springy under my feet. At that moment I made my decision. I just decided to hell with everyone and everything, I will run as I want to.

"I then took control over my running and I did not depend on my coach, family or friends. Suddenly all the pressure lifted and I had energy to physically move the world. And so it happened, I ran a 4:09 at altitude. I not only won the race, but set a new South African junior record. (This is the equivalent of a sub 4:30 mile run by a 15 year-old girl!)

"Looking back on my career, I ran my best races when I took control and ran not because of outcomes, but because I wanted to run. As soon as my running was taken away from me by other people who wanted me to run, I ran very poorly indeed."

When you realize how important your role as a runner is, you take responsibility for the level and quality of running that you produce. In other words, once you realize that your running serves a greater purpose than you initially realized, you make sure that you give of your best when you run. There is more at stake. Your running means more than just your sport to others. By running you serve yourself. A superior level of fitness enhances your quality of life. You are more energetic. You are happier, because you are healthy and in control. Running greatly improves your self-esteem.

In turn, you make those around you happy when you are fit, happy, healthy and fulfilled. You can contribute more at home and in the workplace when you are in good shape. On a larger scale, through your running, you are a balanced, healthy member of society. By being both mentally and physically well you are better able to contribute to society. Consider that you are not a part of the alarming series of statistics on the epidemic of obesity, or man-hours lost to illness annually or any other such problem that daily faces society at large. Now this might sound a little over the top, but consider the motivational impact of having this in mind on days when you find it hard to lace on those running shoes and get out the door. Realize your value to others.

To offer a literal example of this, many of my international-class runners have run their best times in Ekiden races. These are international relay races where runners are part of a team and run for their country. More is at stake than just each runner's own performance, and when they realize this, they give more than they think they have. This is because while they are competing, they are keeping in mind the contribution to others that they are making. Be a member of a team in your family, with your friends and in life. Be a valuable team player, for your sake and the sake of all mankind.

KNOW WHAT YOUR GIFT IS

Your ultimate level of running is not something "out there" that you strive for. It IS each day's running. It is essential to dwell upon this fact each time you run. "I am out here doing that which I love. There is no other place I'd rather be nor any other activity I'd rather be doing right now, than this running."

By saying this to yourself and absorbing its significance, you are serving yourself. After all, you are doing what you choose to be doing. The only thing that stands between you and full enjoyment is failing to be in the moment. When you are fully conscious of the process at the time of its occurrence, there is no room for doubt or fear or failure. Always be aware of what you are giving. Bear this in your own mind and discuss the idea with others, even telling them how you see your running as being a gift to the world.

When those around you see this joy, and realize that they are also being considered when you plan your running, they too are happy and feel served. Imagine this as outgoing ripples in the pool of your life, influencing loved ones, friends, the community and so on. Your running then becomes balanced and wholesome.

"WHEN I RUN, I CONTRIBUTE IN WAYS EVEN BEYOND MY UNDERSTANDING"

SHARING YOUR RUNNING

What does your running need, so that you may feel served?

_____

_____

_____

_____

EXAMPLE: *To enjoy the support of my partner and family, especially on race day.*

In what ways could your running possibly serve those you care about?

_____

_____

_____

_____

EXAMPLE: *When I run, I am happy and healthy. My partner wants both these for me. I am at my best with others when I am fulfilled, and they enjoy my company more.*

How can your running possibly serve others outside your friends and family?

_____

_____

_____

_____

EXAMPLE: *When I run I set an example that others whom I do not directly know might follow. I inspire others to consider a healthy lifestyle. I contribute to the increased health and well being of my community and society as a whole. I provide quality service where I work, because I am fit and have high self-esteem. My passion for running is infectious and enthuses those around me.*

"WHEN I RUN, I CONTRIBUTE IN WAYS
EVEN BEYOND MY UNDERSTANDING"

FURTHER USEFUL HINTS & EXAMPLES

Questions to ask yourself:

Is your running the gift it should be?

What do you gain (on all and any level) from running?

How do you serve those around you through running?

FURTHER EXAMPLES OF WAYS TO VIEW YOUR RUNNING AS A GIFT:

To yourself:

- *When I run I have fun*
- *When I run I enjoy competing*
- *When I run I enjoy the sensation of physical exertion*
- *I enjoy doing something for myself*
- *I am fulfilled and self-realized when I run*
- *I support my self-esteem when I run*
- *I feel proud and confident as a runner*
- *I enjoy my friends*

To others:

- *I'm nice to be around when I'm fit and healthy*
- *When I run I'm fulfilled and seek to provide others that opportunity*
- *When I'm healthy I "add" to the health index of society in general*
- *When I'm fit I provide better quality service where I work*
- *When I'm fit I have more energy to spend quality time with friends and family*
- *I set an example of health, fitness, participation and how to be self-realized to others*

HOW ARE YOU DOING WITH CHAPTER 12?
SHARING YOUR RUNNING

Record the date each time you focus on this component

Date	Date	Date	Date

How do you rate your proficiency with this component?
(Write a date and a score out of five in the block next to the date.)

Rating Scale: 5 = excellent, 4 = good, 3 = acceptable, 2 = poor, 1 = very poor

Date	Score	Date	Score	Date	Score	Date	Score	4 week av.

Comments (Periodically write down any realizations you have in this area. How does being aware that your running is a gift to both yourself and others free you up to completely enjoy your running?)

Date

Date

Date

THIS RUNNING JOURNEY
RUNNING FOR LIFE, RUNNING AS LIFE

*"You've got to work like you're never going
to get paid; dance like nobody's watching;
and love like it's never going to hurt."*
- ANONYMOUS

The purpose of the previous 12 chapters is for you to fully realize what your running and participation in this sport is all about. Your targets are magnets that draw you in the direction you wish to go. Your goals are to assist you in being the runner you want to be and in daily exhibiting the creative behaviors required to reach your targets. When this is the case, then your running enriches your life with joy and fulfillment.

Even if you don't always reach all your targets, your efforts provide you with ample opportunity to fully live your life. After all, even when you do achieve your targets, you simply set new ones anyway. This provides the real momentum for a life of successful endeavor and fulfillment; something that all runners strive for.

Mark Plaatjes, world champion marathon runner, and all-around good guy, says the following regarding the role running plays in his life:

"Running has defined my life as a person, a physical therapist, a dad and also a husband. The way my life goes, is the way my running goes—when I am running well, I am focused, goal oriented, single minded and selfish. This translates into other areas of my life. At work I am sharper and I screw things up less. I have more energy at home to do things with my wife and my children, and in general I am just much more productive in all spheres of my life.

"Running is my passion. It brings passion to everything I do in my life and because of that, my life brings passion to my running."

WHERE YOU'VE COME FROM

Whether you achieve a target on time or not becomes less relevant when you look back upon the road you've traveled. By taking this broader view of your running, you acknowledge all the goals you've achieved in your striving, all the people you've met, and all the opportunities that were uncovered along the way. Notice all the fun and fulfillment you've experienced. Become fully aware of all the quality running you've done and been blessed with.

When you don't look at this bigger picture, what you get out of your running will inevitably shrink. So often running—and so much else that you do—ultimately fails as an endeavor because you focus on running only "in order to...",

For example, "I run so that I can eat anything I want. I run to lose weight. I run because my lover wants me to/is a runner. I run to win. I run to keep fit. I run so that I can be accepted in my community/by my friends."

To have such "in order to's" as targets (Chapter 4) to draw you along through your running life is fine. But to have them as the ultimate pinnacle or reason for your endeavors leaves you open to the reality that anything finite will not satisfy you for long.

If you persist with this approach of limited reasons, chances are you might stop running. Only after you've ceased running will you realize that you had been gaining a whole host of benefits you originally did not notice (you were happy, fulfilled, at peace, stable, energetic, motivated, excited, filled with anticipation and self-realized). It might then occur to you how much you miss the very act of running.

Another doomed "in order to" reason to continue running is in the hope that you will rediscover those golden days when your running seemed to provide so much more. This search for the joy of the past is futile if you remain within the mindset that if you keep running you will find that which you so desperately seek. The running itself is what you seek!

FOCUS ON THE PROCESS

Instead of these limited and limiting reasons to run, focus on the process of running and watch the joy return. By running "so that...," you are essentially not present to the activity itself at the time that you are doing it. You tend to focus on the outcomes you desire and might even consider your running as painful, unpleasant or even a sacrifice "so that" you can get what you want.

All this diminishes the quality of the experience and in essence you lose much of that integral joy and value that running provides. The only true reason to run is because you choose to run! (See the final affirmation of this chapter). We run because we run, all other benefits are secondary and a bonus.

There is a school of thought and strong empirical evidence to suggest that often runners come stuck in their running after 6 to 8 years, as a result of having over-developed their *left brain* running. Although evidence is anecdotal, it has been found that when runners are encouraged to develop their *right brain* approach to running, the joy and satisfaction they formerly experienced returns. It would seem that these focused efforts on being less intent upon time, distance, effort and performance can return runners to a state of balance. It is strongly suggested that you analyze your running in this regard.

LEFT BRAIN "THINKING" IS CHARACTERIZED BY THE FOLLOWING:	RIGHT BRAIN THINKING AND ACTIONS ENTAIL:
being practical and down to earth	being impulsive/intuitive
being active and busy	being relaxed, moving around a little slower, being passive
being results and outcome orientated	spending more quiet time doing nothing structured
being physically/bodily focused	being more spiritual and mind focused
being highly target-oriented	doing activities without specific results in mind
taking on responsibility	spending more time going out and having fun
thinking ahead	being in the moment
logical and analytical thinking	being more creative (painting, writing and other art/hobbies)
being sociable and in the company of people (networking)	spending time alone

If you notice that your running is highly left brain focused, attempt the following to achieve more right brain balance:

- Seek running routes that are peaceful and beautiful, especially where there is water (lakes, rivers or the ocean).

- Run only as a spectator, noticing the beauty and detail of your surroundings. You can run alone or share the beauty and experience with a friend. Narrate to someone how beautiful and enjoyable it was.

- Have some of your runs be as slow as is comfortable and enjoy only the process of your running action.

- Seek quiet, safe routes to run alone.

- Ponder, meditate or pray during some of your easy runs.

- Attempt to run some of your easier sessions without concern for speed, time or distance—focus only on the process of running and see it for what it is—no more (don't interpret or give meaning). Don't wear a watch. Have no purpose or expected outcome.

- While you run imagine you are creating something with your running—like a symphony or a painting that soothes and flows, that blends color and sound and that is something of beauty, balance, rhythm, joy and peace.

If you realize fully that your running provides you with a way through which you can enjoy yourself, a way in which you can perform, a place where you can find friendship, an opportunity to have your deepest needs met, then it really is not about winning or losing, but about having fully lived and totally participated along the way.

If you look for these things in your running, you will find them. Then running IS all worth it.

SELF REALIZATION

The great sociologist Abraham Maslow clearly illustrated the growth of man to fulfillment with his celebrated model of man's "hierarchy of needs." He stated that when the basic human needs of air, safety, food, means, security, love and belonging are met, the final step is to be self-realized or self-actualized. Self-realization and self-actualization are the same concept. They refer to the ultimate pinnacle of human existence, which is to be involved in the process of realizing your life's purpose. To know your life's purpose and to be fulfilling that purpose through the utilization of your potential is to be self-realized or actualized.

When people have all they desire and still feel empty and unfulfilled it is mostly because they have yet to recognize that without being able to serve, and without being constantly challenged, there is no meaning. Being self-realized or self-actualized is man's highest state of being. This occurs when we do things simply to enjoy the process. There is only the challenging of *Self* (the higher, spiritual self), as opposed to the *ego*, and a seeking for personal growth. Activities that you participate in for the purpose of self-realization have no extrinsic reward at stake. You do not get paid for doing them. You do not get praised or honored for them. There is no need for others to see or even know that you do them. Their value is intrinsic and exists in the doing.

There are many ways in which one can distinguish between ego and Self. I like the explanation that suggests that the part of us that is continuously providing commentary on what we are doing; "No! That's wrong, do this, do that, you fool..." and so on, is the ego. The Self is that part of us that is doing the running, or the talking or the other actions that constitute our lives. This Self can also be called the *Spirit*. A further definition is that the ego is subjective, (interpreting), and the spirit objective, (just doing).

To be self-actualized requires you do something for its own reward: For example, you run because you love the process. To fully experience the *doing* as the only purpose is to be self-realized. The reason for life is to live it fully and be present each step of the way.

In your running, even with all the latest equipment, sufficient time to train, great ability, regular PR's and perfect places to run injury free, there still is something lacking unless you are challenged, moving forward, striving and serving.

Richard Bach, author of Jonathan Livingstone Seagull said it all so succinctly when he stated: "Here is a test to find whether your mission on earth is finished: If you're alive it isn't."

NEW CHALLENGES

So too if you are not continually seeking new challenges and new experiences with your running you may soon become bored and disillusioned. There are always new routes to run, distances to run faster, races to run further, friends to meet and compete with, equipment and training to try, nutrition to be improved, lifestyles to be balanced and new feelings and experiences to explore.

It is important to distinguish between "seeking new challenges" in running and running "in order to." The key is to make your targets serve you rather than being a servant to them.

There is limited excitement in the known. Without excitement there is no passion, and without passion there is no real adventure to life, just dour existence. Therefore constantly be seeking the unknown and keep pushing back the limits of your own creation and experience, saying:

- "I can enjoy my running more"
- "I can run faster"
- "I can run longer"
- "I can do more for myself and others through my running"
- "By taking on my running challenges I discover life solutions"
- "Running defines me in the moment"
- "With running my life is more fulfilled"
- "I like who I become through my running"
- "I fulfill some of my life's purpose through running"
- "When I run I am happy"
- "When I run I am fulfilled"
- "Running makes me feel good"
- "I am proud to be a runner"

See that you have what you need to fulfill the lower levels of the hierarchy of needs (see Maslow earlier in this chapter), and then place your focus on the various levels of what it takes to be self-realized as a runner. Then act.

Let me give you an example: I coach many runners of varying abilities. I often ask them about their targets and goals. Very often their answer is that they wish to be like the best runners I coach in their specific event. When I ask the best runners I coach, the same question, they aspire to something greater than they currently are, even if they are the very best in the world at that time! I then ask them to focus on a time in their past when all that they achieved was but a dream. Once they have done this, I ask them if they enjoyed getting to where they are now. Invariably the answer is yes, as most successful runners achieve that success through being passionate and committed to their sport. Life is fun when you are passionate and committed.

IN AFRICA

Being from Africa and coaching African runners, I know what it is for a runner to not have enough money for running shoes, phone calls or even sufficient food to fuel his or her training. These runners often come from areas that are dangerous and their lives are threatened on a regular basis. Even though many of them achieve a level of success, most do not get as far as their physical potential would allow.

As it turns out, the toughness of their circumstances is an advantage: The stakes are much higher! Failure is rewarded by further poverty and hardship. Thus they remain focused and committed to success. If however their basic needs of safety, food, and group-acceptance and support are not met, they as all people would, fail.

It is interesting to note that when these athletes achieve great performances and are well rewarded financially, they typically maintain this level of performance only for a short while. I believe this to be so because of the fact that their efforts were in order to make money, and their circumstances were desperate. Once they began to receive prize money—which sometimes in one race exceeds the wages they would have received for a lifetime of labor—their motivation waned. Very few of these runners continue to run once their performance years are over. Clearly and sadly a case that running for them is, in most cases, purely a question of economics.

It is essential that you view your running as work in progress. It is especially useful to acknowledge that you continually alter that which you require and desire of your running.

THE FOUR RUNNING STAGES

Typically you get into running when you are young, as a competitive activity. You love to race, or you are afraid of races, but you race anyway, because that's why you run when you are young. Actually, many children run so that they can belong. They wish to be "on the team," and will choose an activity where they best fit or have some skill. Once you have become part of that group you strive to physically improve, to master your body and challenge your limitations. You strive to look good and be seen as an accomplished runner. The purpose of your running is all about yourself and challenging yourself on the physical plane. At this stage you might be called an "*athlete*".

In the next stage of your development you might become what could be termed a "*warrior*" runner. You wish to do battle against others, the races, the elements, the courses, the distance, the training. You wish to be tough, tough, tough— here running is an opportunity to be brave, reckless, courageous and heroic.

This phase might pass too, and you could grow to be a "*elder statesman*" of running, where you put together training groups, serve on running club committees, maybe write about the sport, do a bit of coaching at a local high school or on higher levels. Your purpose here is to teach and to share, and give back to running what it gave you.

There is a possible fourth and final stage in this process of moving from a competitive runner to a lifetime runner: You could evolve to the highest level of running, the stage of the "*spirit*" runner. Here you run for running's sake, to be fully in the moment, to continually rediscover and reinvent yourself as a human being, to simply BE running and have no boundaries that distinguish you as a runner, from the process of running. We all have moments somewhere in our running careers when physiology, mind and spirit (aided by endorphins no doubt!) meld into one glorious continuous moment of timelessness and infinity. This is called the "runner's high". It is in these moments that synchronicity is complete and all that you are as a runner is blissfully fulfilled. The spirit runner has no attachment to outcomes and seeks nothing from his or her run other than the experience and freedom of running. These runners run to run, for no other reason, and their philosophy is the Zen-like affirmation, "I run because I run."

NO STAGE IS NECESSARILY BETTER

None of these stages is better than the other-they are simply phases to be recognized and played with.

To remain *the athlete,* continually attempting mastery of your body is perfectly fine. It is a noble, fulfilling and satisfying cause.

To achieve satisfaction from head-to-head competition is perfect too. Challenging yourself by taking on the perceived limits of distance and speed is very pure. Some never tire from the thrill of racing or the opportunities for assertiveness, and why do you need to? Race on!

If serving, coaching and teaching in running inspires you and provides great joy and satisfaction, as they do for so many, why stop? Clearly running plays its biggest role when it serves you fully. There is no better way to enjoy running's full benefit than by serving and teaching. This is essential when the benefits of being of value to the community are at stake.

We all wish to be valued and feel as if we belong and are needed (remember Maslow). There is no better way for us to achieve this state than to serve. To end our running lives in service of the sport that serves us is to leave the greatest legacy. The circle would be complete.

As with all of life, few achieve the permanent level of *spirit* running that is possible. We go in and out and catch/feel glimpses of its serenity. This level of running is not necessarily the logical final step for all runners. There is no "failure" in not reaching, or not even striving to reach this level. If you achieve moments of this state, you should enjoy and cherish them. You should not lose perspective or consider your other levels of running as inferior. They are simply different.

Of greater importance is to fully experience all that occurs in your running life. Remind yourself constantly of this. Say something in the following vein; "Should I not be able to run another step ever again, I will go with peace into whatever lies ahead, for I have filled my allotted running time with all that I wanted from my sport up to this point. There is nothing missing, there is nothing incomplete. I am fulfilled each moment."

These words have two great rewards:

- You take responsibility for each running experience being full and complete, as if it were your last, so that you can say these words.

- By saying and believing these words, you make it so. They become your truth and a glorious and magical one it is too!

Ask yourself, while you are running or racing:

- "Am I enjoying myself?"
- "Have I been forced to be here?"
- "Do I choose to be here?"
- "Am I participating for the right reasons?"
- "Am I serving myself and others by my running?"

Through achieving success and focusing on what you want, your answers to these questions should always be positive. If not, it lies in your hands to correct the matter, to make the right choices so that you can say:

"I AM ON THE RIGHT PATH"

"THE ULTIMATE GOAL IS THE JOURNEY"

SAVORING YOUR RUNNING FOR WHAT IT IS

Continually add to the following list so as to be reminded of the myriad reasons why you run. Remember, as time passes the list will grow. Some points will be deleted, others changed. It is recommended that you refer to it weekly so that you are reminded of why you LOVE to run.

EXAMPLE: *I love how I look when I am running fit.*

_____

_____

_____

_____

_____

EXAMPLE: *I love the cut and thrust of racing.*

_____

_____

_____

_____

_____

EXAMPLE: *I really enjoy coaching those high school kids.*

_____

_____

_____

_____

_____

EXAMPLE: *When I run I am at peace and all that there is, is simple*

physical activity. I am fully in the moment.

_____

_____

_____

_____

FURTHER USEFUL HINTS & EXAMPLES

For your running to ultimately serve you, you need to perceive it as an activity through which you achieve joy, peace, love and happiness. Fulfillment is an ongoing process.

Find the depth of fulfillment from your running that you desire.

Questions to ask yourself:
Are you happy and fulfilled?

If you are not, why not?

By when will you be?

What will it take?

Given that happiness and satisfaction are choices, why are you choosing unhappiness and dissatisfaction?

Do you run to run? Or do you run to "get there"?

Have you realized that no matter how well you run, there will always be something more to achieve?

Has this given you more running freedom?

Would you still run if you had no hope of achieving what you once did or what you once believed you could do? Ponder this.

Do you train to   – enjoy it?
                 – get fit?
                 – ward off disease?
                 – race faster?
                 – win or beat others?
                 – to feel good?

Do you race – to win?

> – to enjoy the event?
> – run a faster time?
> – to be with others of similar interest?
> – to feel good about yourself?

What has running given you?

What do you still expect to receive from your life in and through running?

EXAMPLES OF POSSIBLE ANSWERS:

– *When I run I experience life to the full*
– *Running provides me with an opportunity to further fill my life with a worthwhile activity*
– *When I run I feel my life is working*
– *When I run I experience it as some part of my life's purpose*

HOW ARE YOU DOING WITH CHAPTER 13?
RUNNING FOR LIFE, RUNNING AS LIFE

Record the date each time you focus on this component

Date	Date	Date	Date

How do you rate your proficiency with this component?
(Write a date and a score out of five in the block next to the date.)

Rating Scale: 5 = excellent, 4 = good, 3 = acceptable, 2 = poor, 1 = very poor

Date	Score	Date	Score	Date	Score	Date	Score	4 week av.

Comments   (Periodically write down any realizations you have in this area. How does constantly reminding yourself that the process of running is all there is enhance your enjoyment of the moment? How does detaching from the need to have certain outcomes determine your happiness? Record how distinguishing this raises your running experience to higher levels.)

Date

_____

Date

_____

Date

_____

PUTTING IT ALL TOGETHER
WHAT ARE THE ELEMENTS OF MAGICAL RUNNING?

IN SUMMARY

By SELF EVALUATION (Chapter 3) you determine where you are. By setting TARGETS (Chapter 4) you set aims and objectives that determine the direction or course you intend to follow. By GOALSETTING (Chapter 5) you determine how you wish to remain on that path. Once you know these, you create a MISSION (Chapter 6) by which you are guided through a lifetime of running and individual events. You then continually set the scene for these to become realized through VISUALIZATION (Chapter 7). By recalling past successes you place yourself in the SUCCESS ZONE (Chapter 8). You ensure success by having a well-prepared mental STRATEGY (Chapter 9). Along the way you will meet with CHALLENGES (Chapter 11), and will have CHOICES (Chapter 10) to make. In all this you will see your running as a GIFT (Chapter 12) to yourself and others. You ensure that all this comes to pass by reminding yourself of your commitments through powerful AFFIRMATIONS (Chapter 2). Finally you joyfully realize that it is not about getting to some place specific with your running, but the JOURNEY (Chapter 13) itself.

Now that you have designed your running through each individual chapter, let's do one final creative exercise encompassing all 12 of the skills.

Briefly consider the lessons learned from each of the 12 elements and create an affirmation that will ensure that these remain with you throughout your running life. Don't be afraid to constantly adapt these, as they will grow as your running does. Please refer back to the chapters as you complete the exercises.

Chapter 2   AFFIRMED RUNNING

_____

_____

_____

_____

EXAMPLE: *"My powerful self-talk consistently ensures great running"*

Chapter 3   THE START LINE

_____

_____

_____

_____

EXAMPLE: *"I know where I am with my running and therefore move forward with confidence"*

Chapter 4   SETTING RUNNING TARGETS

_____

_____

_____

_____

EXAMPLE: *"I know what I want and therefore am clear of where my running is taking me and where I want my running to go"*

Chapter 5   RUNNING GOALS

_____

_____

_____

_____

EXAMPLE: *"Each day I am the runner I want to be"*

Chapter 6   A RUNNING MISSION

_____

_____

_____

_____

EXAMPLE: *"With each run I further create a career and experience of which I am proud"*

Chapter 7   VISUALIZED RUNNING

_____

_____

_____

_____

EXAMPLE: *"I see each running success before it happens"*

Chapter 8   THE RUNNING GROOVE

_____

_____

_____

_____

EXAMPLE: *"With each run or race I slip easily into the enjoyment/ success/performance zone"*

Chapter 9   STRATEGIC RUNNING

_____

_____

_____

_____

EXAMPLE: *"My running works, for it is planned"*

Chapter 10   CHOICES TO RUN BY

_____

_____

_____

_____

EXAMPLE: *"I choose successful running"*

Chapter 11   RUNNING UNCHALLENGED

_____

_____

_____

_____

EXAMPLE: *"I powerfully solve my running problems, growing from each new challenge met"*

Chapter 12   RUNNING AS A GIFT

_____

_____

_____

_____

EXAMPLE: *"My running joyously serves me, my family and my friends"*

Chapter 13   THIS RUNNING JOURNEY

_____

_____

_____

_____

EXAMPLE: *"I train/run because I absolutely love it"*

ANNUAL GLOBAL SUMMARY

*"When performance is measured, performance improves,
but when performance is measured and recorded,
the rate of performance increases."*
- THOMAS MONSON

Every four weeks carry over your average self-assessment rating for each component onto this chart to see how your skill and power are growing. The value of attaching a numerical value to each component is to be found within the rhythm, discipline and satisfaction such an exercise provides. Runners are fond of numbers and statistics. This exercise entices you to complete each component until you are happily in the habit of taking charge of your destiny and creating an outstanding, exciting and fulfilling running life.

Create nothing less than magical running.

MONTHS (4-WEEK BLOCKS) INDICATED BY COLUMNS / CHAPTERS INDICATED BY ROWS

	1	2	3	4	5	6	7	8	9	10	11	12	13	Av.
2														
3														
4														
5														
6														
7														
8														
9														
10														
11														
12														
13														

Total Av.

I am convinced that should you have enjoyably applied the principles as laid out in these pages, you will continually unleash the best runner you can be.

I wish you a lifetime of Magical Running.

- BOBBY MC GEE

ABOUT THE AUTHOR

Bobby Mc Gee was born in 1957, at altitude in the mountainous pine forested northeast region of South Africa. Track and cross country running were always his favorite sports while at boarding school. Although he ran a sub 2-minute 800-meters at high school in the 1970's, he wasn't about to set the world alight. He did eventually manage to represent his state for triathlon when triathlon was barely a sport!

Bobby has an Honors degree in Human Movement Studies and gained his masses of practical experience as a high school teacher and coach for 12 years, before traveling the globe in support of athletes pursuing excellence on the world stage.

His first real insight into the evils of apartheid in South Africa came when he, as a white coach, realized the painful irony that the black and "colored" (yes in South Africa there's a difference) athletes that he coached were not allowed to participate internationally because of South Africa's policy of discrimination on the basis of color! Through his coaching he played an important role in the unification of athletics in South Africa, and in South Africa's first appearance in more than 3 decades in the Olympic Games (Barcelona, 1992).

Through his coaching, writing (he is a columnist and technical editor for Runner's World South Africa), and inspirational work, he has become a much sought after figure in the world of human potential fulfillment. Today his efforts are channeled through *Magical Life*, a business specializing in supporting individuals and groups through motivational workshops to give wings to their dreams, both athletic and personal. Together with his partner and long-time friend Tony Longhurst, he has produced numerous courses and seminar/workshops for coaches and runners in the United States and South Africa. His unique and highly effective coaching system and mental skills programs have guided thousands of runners and walkers of varying abilities to achieve their own personal targets and goals.

With the release of *Magical Running* and the increased availability of courses and seminars, he is striving to spread his message even more widely.

He travels between Boulder, Colorado and Cape Town, South Africa, spending time in each country following his own dreams which often involve hours in the mountains working up a sweat and a smile.

SUGGESTED READING LIST

Awaken The Giant Within
Anthony Robbins

Chicken Soup for the Soul (The whole series)
Mark Victor Hansen/Jack Canfield

Man's Search For Meaning
Viktor Frankl

Mind in Sport
Kenneth E Jennings

Mind Power
John Kehoe

Sacred Hoops
Phil Jackson & Hugh Delahunty

The Prophet
Kahlil Gibran

The Psychology of Successful Competing in Endurance Events
Brent S. Rushall & Justice R. Potgieter

The Richest Man in Babylon
George S. Clason

The Seven Spiritual Laws of Success
Deepak Chopra

Think and Grow Rich
Napoleon Hill

You'll See It When You Believe It
Dr. Wayne Dyer

INSPIRING AND MAGICAL

Thank you for reading *Magical Running*. We hope you had as much fun reading it as we did writing it.

Bobby Mc Gee and Magical Life offer a range of seminars, products and educational programs. These include:

Magical Running Seminars
!UNLEASH! Youth Seminar *(High Schools)*

FORTHCOMING TITLES

Magical Running Workbook
The action book that helps to continually create magic in your running.

Letters to Colleen
Inspirational letters from a coach to his athletes. Get the inside scoop on what it takes to motivate Olympians, world record holders, and other runners.

For additional information please contact Magical Life.

Toll free: 877-9-MAGICAL (877-962-4422)
E mail: info@magicalife.com
Fax: 303-527-2784
Website: www.magicalife.com
Mail: Magical Life, P.O. Box 17866, Boulder, CO 80308-0866

FOR ADDITIONAL COPIES OF MAGICAL RUNNING
PLEASE FILL IN THE ORDER FORM ON THE NEXT PAGE
OR VISIT YOUR LOCAL RUNNING OR BOOK STORE

TO ORDER MORE MAGICAL RUNNING

Telephone orders: Toll free **1-877-9 MAGICAL** (877-962-4422)
Please have your Visa or Mastercrd ready.

Fax orders: 303-527-2784

Online orders: www.magicalife.com

Postal orders: P.O. Box 17866, Boulder, CO 80303-0866

Please send me _____ copies of this book (indicate quantities).

I understand that I may return any books for a full refund—for any reason.

Name: _____ Date:_____

Address:_____

City:_____State:_____ Zip:_____

Telephone:_____Fax:_____

E-mail:_____

❑   Please include me on your mailing list for further information about products and services.

Sales tax: Colorado residents please add State & City tax.

Shipping. US - $4.00 for the first book, $2.00 for each book thereafter
Overseas - International rates apply

Payment: ❑ Check (make checks payable to Magical Life LLC)   Credit card: ❑ Master Card ❑ Visa

My card number is: _____

Name on card:_____

Expiration date:_____

Signature:_____

# Books ____ **x $17.95**	
Tax	
Shipping	
TOTAL	

CALL TOLL FREE AND ORDER NOW

NOTES